PONTIFICIA UNIVERSITAS SANCTAE CRUCIS
FACULTAS IURIS CANONICI

Aloysius ENEMALI

THE
FORMAL
REQUIREMENTS
OF THE
CELEBRATION
OF MARRIAGE:

A Comparative Study of Canon Law,
Nigeria Statutory Law and Nigeria
Customary Law

Thesis *ad Doctoratum in Iure Canonico*
Partim edita

ROMAE 2009

Order this book online at www.trafford.com
or email orders@trafford.com

Most Trafford titles are also available at major online book retailers.

Printed in the United States of America.

ISBN: 978-1-4907-0914-7 (sc)
ISBN: 978-1-4907-0913-0 (e)

Trafford rev. 07/17/2013

 www.trafford.com

North America & international
toll-free: 1 888 232 4444 (USA & Canada)
fax: 812 355 4082

Vidimus et adprobavimus ad normam statutorum

Prof. Dr. Paulus Gefaell
Prof. Dr. David Cito

Imprimi potest

Prof. Dr. Aloisius Ph. Navarro
Decanus Facultatis Iuris Canonici

Dr. Emmanuel Miedes
Secretarius Generalis Universitatis

Roma, 19/11/2008
Prot. N* 452/2008

Imprimatur

Con approvazione ecclesiastica
Dal Vicariato di Roma
S.E. Mons. Luigi Moretti
Arcivescovo tit. Di Mopta
Vicereggente
Roma, 26/01/2009

TABLE OF CONTENTS

CHAPTER TWO: OBSERVATIONS, COMPARISONS,
AND PROPOSALS

ACKNOWLEDGEMENT

Life is good. But nothing is good in life if God did not give it to us. I wish to express my gratitude in the first place to God the author of our life. He is the one that made all things possible. My thanks also go to the Blessed Virgin Mother of Our Lord Jesus Christ and Mother of all priests for her intercessions.

I thank in a special way my first and second moderators Prof. Dr. Pablo Gefaell and Prof. Dr. Miguel Angel Ortiz for their exemplary life. Both were very encouraging and fatherly. I thank all the members of the faculty and students of Canon Law at the Holy Cross University Rome. All the Professors and members of the staff were very kind and patient with me. I thank the Rector, the Secretary General and the Chaplain of the University for their Constant Guidance and help. I thank the Holy Cross Foundation in Austria for providing the scholarship that enabled me to do licentiate study in Canon Law.

I thank Francis Cardinal Arinze and Msgr.Denis Isizoh for their brotherly advice. I thank the Archbishop emeritus of Onitsha Archdiocese, Most Rev. Dr. Albert K. Obiefuna for giving me the opportunity to study law at the University of Lagos and the Nigerian Law School. I thank my Current Ordinary, Most Rev. Dr. Valerian M. Okeke for his confidence in me and for sending me to study Canon Law in Rome.

I thank my parent, chief and Mrs. Emanuel Enemali for their love, care, concern and for encouraging my vocation to the sacred priesthood. I thank all my siblings for their constant support and prayers. I thank my benefactor and his wife, Chief and Mrs. Louis Onwugbenu for their constant support. I thank my numerous friends among who are Chief and Mrs. B. Ebong, Mrs. M. Jordan, Dr. G. Golden, Colonel. P. Brady, Chief B. Amuta, John, Sheila and Dawn Wheaton, Mrs.R. Glenn, Attorney B. Winnermore, Frs. E. Anyadike, F. Oborji, A. Ibegbunam, M. Banjo, P. Ijasan D. Williamson, and other brother priests for their friendship and support. Lastly, I remain grateful to you all who in one way or the other have contributed to the success of this work.

ABBREVIATIONS

AAS	Acta Apostolicae Sedis
AC	Appeal Cases, English Law Reports
ALL E.R	All England Reports (English)
ALL N.L.R	All Nigeria Law Reports
ASS	Acta Sanctae Sedis
BPS	Benue—Plateau State
C.	Canon
CC	Canons
C.C	Customary Court
CCEO	Codex Canonum Ecclesiarum Orientalium
Cap	Capitolo (Chapter)
CIC	Codex Iuris Canonici (Code of Canon Law)
Cod	The code of Justinian
D	The digest of Justinian
Ed(s)	Editor (s)
ECSLR	East Central State Law Reports (Nigeria)
ENLR	Eastern Nigerian Law Reports
ER	English Reports
Et.al	Et alia (and others)
Etc	Et cetera (and so forth)
FLC	Federal Law Court; Law Reports (Australia)
FNR	Federation of Nigeria Law Report
HL	House of Lords; Law Report s (English)

Ibid	Ibidem (The same work/place)
ISLR	Imo State Law Report
J	Judge
LRPD	Law Reports Probate Division (English)
MA	Marriage Act (Nigeria)
MCA	Matrimonial Causes Act (Nigeria)
MCR	Matrimonial Causes Rules (Nigeria)
No	Number
NLR	Nigeria Law Reports
NNLR	Northern Nigeria Law Reports
NMLR	Nigeria Monthly Law Reports
NWLR	Nigeria Weekly Law Reports
PG	Patrologiae Cursus Completus, Series Graeca
PL	Patrologiae Cursus Completus, Series Latina
P	Page
Pp	Pages
Pt	Part
RRD	Romae Rotae Decisiones
S	Section
SC	Judgment of the Supreme Court of Nigeria
SCPF	Sacra Congregatio de Propaganda Fide
SRRD	Sacrae Romanae Rotae Decisiones seu Sententiae
SS	Sections
Vol	Volume
WLR	Weekly Law Reports (English)
WNLR	Western Nigeria law reports
§	Paragraph
§§	Paragraphs

GENERAL INTRODUCTION

M arriage is an important institution in human history. It is the foundation of the family which is the nucleus of the society. It is established by the consent of the parties, which cannot be supplied by any human power.[1]

For the marital consent of the parties to create a marriage, however, the parties must be legally capable[2] and the consent must be lawfully manifested.[3]

The formal requirement of the celebration of marriage deals with the lawful manifestation of the marital consent. It tells how consent could be lawfully exchanged in order to bring about marriage recognized in any given society, be it the Church, the State or the tribal communities. It settles issues such as: Where, when and before

---

[1] *Codex Juris Canonici,* Auctoritate Joannis Pauli II promulgatus, January 25, 1983: AAS 75 (1983) 11, pp. 1-301, c. 1057 § 1 (This work shall here after be refereed to as *CIC 1983*).

[2] *CIC 1983*, c. 1057 § 1.Legal capability here means absence of matrimonial impediment such as found in canons 1083-1094 of this code. In addition the parties must not be incapable to contract marriage due to emotional or psychological conditions as seen in canon 1095 of this code.

[3] Ibid.

whom could marital consent be exchanged? What is the formula for the exchange of marital consent? Etc.

The Church, the State and the customary tribes in Nigeria have laws that govern this formal requirement for the celebration of acceptable marriage. It is the aim of this thesis to examine these laws pointing out their differences and similarities.

Motivation

There are in Nigeria several judicial decisions that consider marriage in the Roman Catholic Church as mere Church blessing of the customary marriage or the statutory marriage. Church marriage,[4] as it were does not have an independent existence under the Nigerian law. I was therefore moved to examine the form of the celebration of marriage in the code of canon law in line with the statutory law and the customary law provisions in Nigeria. The purpose of doing this is to establish the striking similarities and differences in the formation of marriage celebrated in the Church and those celebrated in accordance with the statutory and the customary laws in Nigeria. Doing this I hope will enable us to establish a case for a direct recognition of canonical marriage in Nigeria without the complications and repetitions involved in the celebration following the requirements of the customary law and the statutory law.

Scope

This work is limited only to the formal requirements of the celebration of marriage as found in the Church law, the Nigeria statutory law and the Nigeria customary law. The relevant sections

---

[4] We mean by Church marriage here marriage celebrated in accordance with the provision of the canon law. It will from time to time also be referred to as canon law marriage or canonical marriage.

of the code of canon law examined are canons 1108-1123 &1127 of the 1983 Latin code and canons 828-842 of the 1990 Eastern code. These are the central canons on the form of the celebration of marriage in the Church. Equally considered are the Nigerian Marriage Statutes and the customary practices dealing with the formation of marriage in Nigeria.

Methodology

In the preparation of this work, we used the historical, expository, analytical, juridical and comparative methods. The historical method was used because it is necessary to know the foundation and the subsequent development of the law governing the form of the celebration of marriage. The use of the expository method is to help us lay bare the provisions of the laws on our topic. The analytical and the juridical methods were used to critically examine the text of the law in line with its demands on the people. The comparative method was used to match the three laws under consideration in order to pin point their specific areas of congruence and convergence.

Scheme of work

This whole thesis is divided into four main chapters. Each chapter is devoted to a specified area of our discussion.

Chapter one deals with the historical development of the legislation on the form of the celebration of marriage in the Church. This chapter has two sections.

The first section handles the form of the celebration of marriage prior to the ecumenical council of Trent in 1563. It considers the practice adopted in marriage celebrations among the Jews as the forerunners of Christianity and among the Romans as the empire state where Christianity developed into an established religion. It also discusses marriage practices among the early Germanic people and earlier converts to Christianity. The practice among the early Christians of involving their priests in the celebration of marriage was noted. Also noted is the prohibition of secret marriages, which involve the exchange of marital consent not witnessed by the Church officials.

The second section of chapter one talks about the celebration of marriage from the council of Trent (1563) to the present time. It considers the council of Trent and its promulgation of the revolutionary decree *Tametsi* which established for the first time an invalidating canonical form of the celebration of marriage in the Church. Later modifications of the decree by the Benedictine declaration and the decree *Ne Temere* were considered. The provisions of the *1917 code of Canon Law* on the canonical form and the interventions between the code and the Vatican II ecumenical council were equally looked into. Lastly the input of the Vatican II council which culminated in the current canonical form found in the 1983 Latin code and the 1990 Eastern code were considered.

Chapter two delves into the current law of the Church on the form of the celebration of marriage. This in turn has two sections.

The first section talks about the canonical form in the 1983 Latin code. It focuses on canons 1108-1123 &1127. The central message of this section is to establish the canonical form as laid down in the 1983 code, which is simply this: that a valid canonical or Church marriage must be celebrated before an official witness of the church and at least two other witnesses. A detailed discussion on who could serve as official witness of the Church is given. Also, extensive deliberations on those bound and those exempted from the canonical form is equally given. The place of celebration and the fact of the record of the marriage as well as the extraordinary form for the celebration of marriage without an official witness were highlighted.

The second section takes over the issue of the canonical form in the 1990 Eastern code of canon law. Attention was paid particularly to canons 828-842 of the code. An analysis of those who serve as official witness under the Eastern tradition was given. The place of celebration, the record of celebration and the extraordinary form of celebration were equally treated.

Chapter three situates our topic within the Nigerian context. This chapter like the others has two segments.

The first section talks about the statutory laws on marriage. It begins with a brief description of the meaning of statutory law in Nigeria and the Nigerian statutes on marriage. It provides the basic features of marriage celebrated under the statute law before delving into the statutory form of the celebration of marriage. In the preliminary observations, it notes that for the purpose of the statutory marriage in Nigeria, the following provisions of the law must be borne in mind, namely: the marriage districts; the marriage Registrar; the Registrar's office; the licensed place of worship; and the Minister of Religion. These are key information in the celebration of marriage under the statute. Equally noted are the notice of marriage, the Registrar's certificate or the Minister's license to marry and possible objections to the marriage. The place for the celebration of the statutory marriage and the form to be observed were highlighted. Persons bound to celebrate marriage under the statutes and the fact of the record of the celebration of the marriage was noted. Lastly, some judicial proceedings dealing with the form of the celebration of marriage were pinpointed.

The section two of Chapter three treats the customary form of the celebration of marriage. It begins with explaining the meaning of customary law in Nigeria and the nature of marriage under it. Then after, it delves into the formalities for the celebration of marriage in accordance with the customary practices in Nigeria. It notes the fact of the preliminary enquiry which must precede every customary marriage celebration. The three vital elements in the celebration of the customary marriage namely, the public manifestation of consent, the giving and the accepting of the "marriage token"[5] and the formal handing over of the bride to the groom were discussed extensively. The registration and proof of customary marriage were equally discussed. Also considered were the other types of customary marriages in Nigeria and their incidences.

Chapter four, the last of the chapters is meant to be the central focus of our thesis. This chapter is captioned: Observations, comparisons and proposals. It has four numbers.

The number one talks about the reasons for the establishment of the canonical form, the statutory form and the customary form of marriage. It questions the rationale for the introduction of invalidating formal requirements of the celebration of marriage in the three legal systems under consideration. It deduced its reasoning from the facts presented in the three previous chapters.

The number two of chapter four concentrates on the basic similarities and dissimilarities in the canonical, statutory and customary form of marriage celebrations.

The number three deals exclusively with the problems encountered by individual Nigerian Catholics who have to observe the three forms in the celebration of their marriage. As members of the customary community, the Catholics in Nigeria observe the customary form. Being Catholics of the Holy Roman Catholic Church, they are under

---

5   By "marriage token" We mean something money or money worth agreed upon by the families of the parties to a customary law marriage and presented by the groom's family to the bride's family upon acceptance of which by the bride's family the customary marriage is sealed.

obligation to keep the canonical form. But since the canonical form without fulfilling the requirements of the statutory law is of no legal consequence in Nigeria, the Catholic is compelled to observe also the provisions of the *Marriage Act* for the celebration of his marriage. When all these forms are observed one begins to wonder what should be the proper law that should govern the marriage so formed? This is a big problem for the Nigerian Catholics entering into marriage.

The number four and the last number here attempts a solution to the problem. It begins by showing the impossibility of establishing a uniform form of marriage celebration in Nigeria. It gives the reasons for this impracticality among which are the fact that each of these marriages involved have different characteristics and lawmakers. It goes ahead to propose that the way out is the direct civil recognition of canonical marriage. In doing this, it had a literature review of the suggestions of eminent legal professors in Nigeria. It gave the reasons why this proposal is the best that could be achieved. The reasons among others numbered the pluralistic nature of the Nigerian society, the freedom of religion guaranteed by the constitution of the Federal Republic of Nigeria, and the obvious advantages among which is the clarity of law that will be achieved.

The present extract contains chapter three and four, the general conclusion, bibliography, appendices and the table of contents of the entire thesis. The chapter three is here placed as chapter one while the chapter four is placed as chapter two.

CHAPTER ONE

THE NIGERIA STATUTORY AND CUSTOMARY LAW ON THE FORM FOR THE CELEBRATION OF MARRIAGE

In this chapter, which is the extract of chapter three of the entire thesis, we intend to discuss the form for the celebration of marriage recognized by the law in Nigeria. Under the Nigerian Law, there are two recognized types of marriages. These are marriage under the statutory law (statutory or court marriage) and marriage under the customary law (customary law marriage). Section one of this chapter shall handle the statutory marriage, while section two will deal with the customary marriage.

SECTION ONE
THE STATUTORY FORM IN NIGERIA

1.1.1 MEANING OF NIGERIA STATUTORY LAW

The term Statutory Law means "the body of law derived from the statutes rather than from the constitution or judicial decisions"[6]

---

[6] Garner, B.A., et al (eds.), *Black's Law Dictionary*, 7th ed. (Minnesota: West Publishing Co., 1999), p. 1424.

A statute on the other hand is defined as "the act of parliament."[7] Parliament is denominated as "the sovereign legislative authority in the constitution."[8] From the fore going, one could say that statutory law is the legislative act or enactment of the supreme legislative authority in the constitution.

In Nigeria the word statute is stretched to embrace "Ordinances", "Acts", "Laws", "Decrees" and "Edicts".[9]

The word "Ordinance" is used to designate the laws enacted by the Nigerian central government before the first constitution that introduced two tiers of government (federal and regional) on October 1st 1954. Prior to this constitution, Nigeria has only one central government, which was introduced after the amalgamation of the Northern and Southern protectorate on January 1st 1914.

After this first constitution, the word "Acts" was used to designate enactments made or deemed to have been made by the federal legislature. While the word "Laws" was used to refer to the enactments made or deemed to have been made by the regional legislature.[10]

The words "decrees" and "edicts" find their way in the legal vocabulary of Nigeria with the emergence of military rule. On January 15th 1966 the first military coup took place in Nigeria toppling the civilian federal and regional governments.

---

[7] Rutherford, L., & Bones, S. (eds.), *Osborn's Concise Law Dictionary*, (London: Sweet & Maxwell, 1993), p. 310.

[8] Ibid. p. 241.

[9] Obilade, A.O., *The Nigerian Legal System*, (Ibadan: Spectrum Books Ltd., 2001), p. 64.

[10] See the scheduled to the Nigerian (Constitution) Order in Council that introduced the federal Constitution.

Under the military rule, "Decrees" were used to refer to enactments made or deemed to have been made by the federal military government; while "Edicts" were used to refer to those made or deemed to have been made by the regional administrators.

On October 1st 1979 when the military handed over power to civilians, the words "Acts" and "Laws" replaced "Decrees" and "Edicts" respectively. But with another military coup on December 31st 1983 the words "Decrees" and "Edicts" find their way back until dropped on May 29th 1999 when civilians once again came into power.

Following from the above elucidation, a statute in Nigeria could mean an enactment or enactments of the federal legislature and those deemed to have been enacted by it. A statute in Nigeria could also mean an enactment or enactments of the regional (or state) legislatures and those deemed to have been enacted by them.

The term "Nigerian Statutory law" therefore implies laws given either by the federal legislature or the regional (or state) legislatures.

1.1.2 NIGERIAN STATUTES ON MARRIAGE

Nigeria has two statutes on marriage, namely, the Marriage Act[11] and the Matrimonial Causes Act.[12]

The Marriage Act was first promulgated as the Marriage Ordinance 1914 by the central legislature, which emerged from the amalgamation of the Northern and Southern Protectorate that same year. This Marriage Ordinance of 1914 repealed earlier legislations on marriage

---

[11] "The Marriage Act," in *Laws of the Federation of Nigeria 1990,* cap. 218 (this Act shall here after be referred to as MA).

[12] "The Matrimonial Causes Act," in *Laws of the Federation of Nigeria 1990,* cap.220 (this Act shall here after be referred to as MCA).

and became the sole law that regulates the formation and celebration of statutory marriage in Nigeria. In 1961 with the designation of the Ordinance Act of the same year, the Marriage Ordinance evolved into the Marriage Act.

The Matrimonial Causes Act came into being on March 17, 1970 as Matrimonial Causes Decree. This Act in section 114 (1) defined "Matrimonial Causes" to mean:

(a) "Proceedings for a decree of (i) dissolution of marriage, (ii) nullity of marriage; (iii) judicial separation; (iv) restitution of conjugal rights; or (v) jactitation of marriage;

(b) Proceedings for a declaration of the validity of the dissolution or annulment of a marriage by decree or otherwise or of a decree of judicial separation, or for a declaration of the continued operation of a decree of judicial separation, or for an order discharging a decree of judicial separation;

(c) Proceedings with respect to the maintenance of a party to the proceedings, settlements, damages in respect of adultery, the custody or guardianship of infant children of the marriage or the maintenance, welfare, advancement or education of children of the marriage, being proceedings in relation to concurrent, pending or completed proceedings of a kind referred to in paragraph (a) or (b) of this subsection, including proceedings of such a kind pending at, or completed before, the commencement of this Act;

(d) Any other proceedings (including proceedings with respect to the enforcement of a decree, the service of process or costs) in relation to concurrent, pending or completed proceedings of a kind referred to in paragraph (a), (b), or (c) of this subsection, including proceedings of such a kind pending at, or completed before, the commencement of this Act; or

(e) Proceedings seeking leave to institute proceedings for a decree of dissolution of marriage or judicial separation, or proceedings in relation to proceedings seeking such leave".

Prior to 1970, the English law on Matrimonial Causes was applied in Nigeria.[13] The Matrimonial Causes Act, 1970 in Nigeria lean heavily for its materials on similar enactments from other common law countries such as "the Matrimonial Causes Act," 1959 of Australia and "the Divorce Reform Act," 1969 of England, adapting them to the Nigerian situation.[14]

These two Acts regulates statutory marriage in Nigeria. The Marriage Act provides for the necessary requirements for valid celebration of marriage. While the Matrimonial Causes Act governs the incidence of marriages celebrated in accordance with the Marriage Act.

1.1.3 MARRIAGE UNDER THE MARRIAGE STATUTES— BASIC FEATURES.

Marriage entered into in accordance with the rules laid down in the above marriage statutes is called "statutory marriage" or at times referred to as "court marriage."[15] Its basic feature is that it is essentially monogamous and it is established only between one man and one woman. This is in line with the divine-natural law on marriage. God willed marriage between one man (Adam) and one woman (Eve) (Genesis, 1 & 2).

---

[13] See "The State Court (Federal Jurisdiction) Act", s.4, in *Laws of the Federation and Lagos 1958,* cap. 177.

[14] Adesanya, S.A., *Laws of Matrimonial Causes,* (Ibadan: Ibadan University press, 1973), p. 2.

[15] Nwogugu, E.I., *Family Law in Nigeria,* (Ibadan: Claerianum press, 1974), pp. 36-37.

A definition of statutory-monogamous marriage given by Lord Penzance in the famous case of *Hyde v Hyde*[16] as ". . . the voluntary union for life of one man and one woman to the exclusion of all others" is adopted in Nigeria. Accordingly, *the Nigerian Interpretation Act 1964* defines statutory-monogamous marriage as "a marriage which is recognized by the law of the place where it is contracted as a voluntary union of one man and one woman to the exclusion of all others during the continuance of the marriage."[17]

In the above definitions, one can identify three vital elements that constitute a monogamous-statutory marriage. These are "voluntary union", "union for life" and "union of one man and one woman to the exclusion of all others."

The word "voluntary" in law means, "done by design or intention; unconstrained by interference; not impelled by outside influence."[18] In relation to marriage, the word 'voluntary' excludes any element of coerced marriage consent expressed under force or fear, which vitiates the internal freedom of the contracting party. Voluntary union therefore requires that the consent of the parties be mutually, freely and unconditionally exchanged in order to constitute the efficient cause of matrimony. Marital jurisprudence is clear on the established position that in the case of a procedurally proven lack of free consent of any of the parties to a given marriage that purported marriage is declared null and void and of no legal effect.[19]

The union apart from being voluntary must be a "union for life." This could mean nothing but that the union is indissoluble until

---

[16]   *Hyde v Hyde,* LRPD, (1886), p.133.

[17]   "The Interpretation Act, 1964", in *Laws of the Federation of Nigeria, 1990,* cap. 192, s.18.

[18]   Garner, B.A., *Blacks Law dictionary,* op. cit., p. 1569.

[19]   Okpaloka, E.P., *Legal Protection of Marriage and the Family Institutions,* (Onitsha:Trinitas Publications, 2002), p. 174.

the death of either spouse. In view of the civil court however, the phrase "union for life" as seen in the definitions above does not connote indissolubility. It simply means that at the time of the union, the couple or parties must intend the marriage to last for life unless otherwise dissolved by following the due process of the law or by death of either party. In other words, apart from death of either party, a competent court could dissolve the marriage union. This is in sharp contrast with the practice and teachings of the Church on monogamous union, which is regarded as indissoluble by any other force or power except by death of either spouse (Matthew, 19:6).[20]

The union must be between one man and one woman. It is between persons of the opposite sex. "Sex constitutes an essential determination of marriage."[21] Nigeria statutory marriage takes place between a male and a female person.

The union is to the "exclusion of all others". It does not admit polygamy. The husband cannot take another wife during the subsistence of the marriage. The wife cannot also marry another husband during the subsistence of the marriage. The law punishes anyone who during the subsistence of a statutory monogamous marriage attempts to marry another wife[22]

---

[20] ". . . what God has united, human beings must not divide", See also *CIC 83,* c.1056.

[21] Clemens, A.H., "Marriage" in *the New Catholic Encyclopaedia,* vol. 9 (Chicago: Chicago University press, 1990), p. 258.

[22] MA. s.33 (1), forbids the practice; MA s.46, makes it an offence punishable with five years in prison. Criminal Code, in *Laws of the Federation of Nigeria, 1990,* cap. 77, s. 370, create the offence of bigamy punishable with seven years in prison. Also see the cases of *Obele Iliya v Obele* reported in NMLR, 1(1973), pt. 155; and *R v Princewell* reported in NNLR; (1963), pt. 54.

1.1.4 FORM FOR THE CELEBRATION OF MARRIAGE UNDER THE STATUE

1.1.4.1 PRELIMINARY OBSERVATIONS

For the purpose of marriage under the statute of marriage in Nigeria, the following points must be noted:

1. Marriage districts.
2. Marriage Registrars.
3. Marriage/Registrars Offices
4. Licensing of Places of Worship.
5. Minister of Religion.

1.1.4.1.1 MARRIAGE DISTRICTS

District' means "a territorial area into which a country, state, county, municipality, or other political subdivision is divided for judicial, political, electoral, or administrative purposes."[23] In the Marriage Act of Nigeria, 'district' means a marriage district constituted under the Act.[24]

The Marriage Act empowers the President of Nigeria[25] to divide the country into marriage districts by means of an order published in the

---

[23] Garner, B.A, *Blacks Law Dictionary*, op.cit., p. 489; Gove P. B. et al. (eds.), *Webster's third new international dictionary* (Cologne: K.V.MBH publishers, 1993), p.660.

[24] MA s.2

[25] The President of Nigeria here could mean any one at the head of government in Nigeria. During most of the Military Regimes in Nigeria, the office of the president was referred to as that of the Heads of States. By inference, a head of state could perform all the functions designated for the president under the Marriage Act.

Federal Gazette.[26] He may also from time to time with similar order equally published alter the districts.[27]

The criterion for the division of Nigeria into marriage districts is territorial. This implies that every subject of Nigeria living in the country lives within a given marriage district. These districts then form the basis for the celebration of statutory marriage in Nigeria.

1.1.4.1.2 MARRIAGE REGISTRARS

Registrar means "a person who keeps official records."[28] For the purpose of marriage, a registrar will be one who keeps the official record of marriage celebrations and other incidences of marriage.

The Marriage Act provides for the office of the principal registrar; the registrar and the deputy registrar. "There may from time to time be appointed a fit and proper person to be the principal registrar of marriages. There may likewise be appointed a fit and proper person to be the registrar of marriages for each marriage district; also appoint a deputy registrar of marriages for any district to act in the absence or during the illness or incapacity of the registrar." [29]

A registrar is appointed for each marriage district. A deputy registrar is also appointed for each marriage district. The deputy registrar acts in the absence or during the illness or incapacity of the registrar.

---

[26] MA s. 3.

[27] MA s. 3 & "Marriage (Designation of Districts)" Order No. 73, *Laws of Nigeria, 1971.*

[28] Garner, B.A., *Blacks Law dictionary*, op. cit., p. 1288.

[29] MA s. 4 (1), (2), & "Marriage (Appointment of Principal Registrar, Registrars, etc.)", Notice, No. 72 *Laws of Nigeria, 1971.*

1.1.4.1.3 MARRIAGE/REGISTRAR'S OFFICES

The Act made provision for the registrar's offices or marriage offices within every marriage district. This is to be the place earmarked for the purpose by the Minister within any given marriage district.[30] At the moment the registrar's office are found in every local government area of the federation. The office of the principal registrar shall also be the place provided for by the Minister.[31] At the moment the principal registrar's office are found in every state of the federation.

1.1.4.1.4 LICENSING OF PLACES OF WORSHIP

Places of worship in Nigeria are licensed for the purpose of statutory marriage. Unless a place of worship is licensed it may not serve any purpose with respect to marriage under the Act. The Marriage Act empowers the Minister to license any place of worship to be a place for the celebration of marriage with a publication made in the Federal Gazette.[32] The Minister may revoke or cancel such license with similar publications in the Federal Gazette.[33] Places of worship licensed under any enactment repealed by the Act shall be deemed licensed under this Act unless cancelled by the Minister.[34] The practice in Nigeria today is to have main Churches within any given Catholic parish licensed. The Station Churches not licensed may not be used for the celebration of marriages.

1.1.4.1.5 MINISTER OF RELIGION

By minister of religion under the Act is meant any person who is recognized by a given religious group or body as their official

---

[30] MA s.5 & "Marriage (Location of Marriage Offices)" Directions, No. 74, *Laws of Nigeria,* 1971.

[31] Ibid.

[32] MA s. 6 (1).

[33] ibid.

[34] MA s. 6 (2).

minister. The recognition of an individual as a minister of religion is entirely the business of the individual religious groups, bodies or denominations. The Law does not impose this on any group. It is these ministers of religion who could assist at statutory marriages within the given religious group or denomination. A minister of religion in one religious denomination cannot officiate at a statutory marriage within another body of which he/she is not a recognized minister of religion. A Catholic priest for example, cannot officiate at a marriage in an Anglican license place of worship and vice versa.

Seen as ministers of religion under the Act are Roman Catholic priests, Anglican pastors, pastors of registered Pentecostal Churches etc.

1.1.4.2 PRELIMINARY FORMALITIES

Prior to the actual celebration of marriage under the statutes, certain essential preliminary formalities must be put in place. Among such preliminaries to be observed we note the following:

1. Notice of Marriage
2. Registrar's certificate or Minister's license to marry
3. Objections to marriage.

1.1.4.2.1 NOTICE OF MARRIAGE

This is a notice given to the general public of the intended marriage. The purpose of the notice is to prevent the celebration of marriage that is legally objectionable. With respect to this notice the Marriage Act provides that whenever any person intends to marry, one of the parties to the intended marriage should approach any Marriage Registrar in any district and apply to complete and sign the notice made out in a prescribed Form.[35] There are separate Forms for literate

---

[35] MA s.7.

and illiterate parties.[36] These Forms should be provided the parties free of charge.[37] Upon the completion and signing of the Form, the parties shall submit them to the registrar of marriage in the marriage district they wish to have their marriage celebrated.[38]

The registrar of marriage at the intended place of celebration, upon the receipt of the form shall enter its details in the Marriage Notice Book.[39]

The Marriage Notice Book is open to inspection by the general public during the office hours.[40] The notice form itself will be displayed on the outer door or public notice board of the registrar's office. It shall remain so displayed until the registrar issues the certificate to marry or at the expiration of three months.[41]

1.1.4.2.2 THE REGISTRAR'S CERTIFICATE OR THE MINISTER'S LICENCE TO MARRY

The registrar's certificate to marry is a document issued by the registrar to the parties of the intended marriage in a prescribed form indicating that the parties are free to marry.[42] The registrar may issue the certificate twenty-one days after the publication of the Notice or three months from the date of the Notice, upon payment of the prescribed fee.[43]

---

[36] Form A first Schedule to the Marriage Act for literate parties; Form B first schedule to the Marriage Act for illiterate parties, also see MA s. 8.

[37] MA s. 9.

[38] MA s.7.

[39] MA s. 10.

[40] Ibid.

[41] Ibid.

[42] The Prescribed Form is Form C first schedule in the appendix; See also MA s.7.

[43] MA s. 11.

The Registrar shall not issue the certificate unless satisfied by affidavit to the effect that

   (a) "One of the parties has been resident within the district in which the marriage is intended to be celebrated for at least fifteen days preceding the grant of the certificate.

   (b) Each of the parties to the intended marriage (not being a widower or widow) is twenty-one years old or that if he or she is under that age, the consent hereinafter made requisite has been obtained in writing and is annexed to such affidavit.

   (c) There is not any impediment of kindred or affinity, or any other lawful hindrance to the marriage.

   (d) Neither of the parties to the intended marriage is married by Customary Law to any person other than the person with whom such marriage is proposed to be contracted."[44]

The Affidavit in question may be sworn before a Registrar, or before an Administrative Officer, or before recognized Minister of Religion.[45] It is the statutory duty of the person receiving the deposition of the affidavit to explain to the person making the affidavit the prohibited degrees of consanguinity and affinity; the penalty imposed for contracting marriage with a third party under the Act while validly married to another person under Native Law and Custom; or for contracting marriage under Customary Law when already married under the Act. Willful failure to give this explanation is an offence punishable with two years imprisonment.[46] The person taking the affidavit shall sign a declaration written thereupon; that the above explanations have been given and that the deponent of the affidavit appeared to fully understand it.[47]

---

[44]   MA s. 11 (1) (a-d),
[45]   MA s.11 (2).
[46]   MA.s.11 (3).
[47]   MA.s.11 (4).

The Registrar's certificate and the procedure for obtaining it can be dispensed and replaced with the Minister's License to marry. The Marriage Act provides "the Minister upon proof being made to him by affidavit that there is no lawful impediment to the proposed marriage, and that the necessary consent, if any, to such marriage has been obtained, may, if he shall think fit, dispense with the giving of notice, and with the issue of the certificate of the Registrar, and may grant his license, which shall be according to Form D in the First Schedule, authorizing the celebration of marriage between the parties named in such license by a Registrar, or by a recognized Minister of Religion of some religious denomination or body"[48]

Reference to the Minister here calls for the question, who is meant by the Minister in Section 13 of the Marriage Act? Academic authors of legal repute are of the view that the Minister here refers to the "the Governors of a State",[49] or "the Military Governor or Administrator of a State"[50]

There are varied situations that could warrant the granting of the Minister's License. An instance is where the parties cannot wait for the twenty-one days period to place a notice with the Registrar of Marriage. Another situation is where a public figure wants to contract marriage quietly without much publicity.

The Registrar's certificate or the Minister's License must be obtained before any celebration of Statutory Marriage in Nigeria. Any one who officiates at Marriage in violation of this provision is guilty of a crime and liable to five years in jail.[51]

---

[48] MA s.13.
[49] Nwogugu, E.I., *Family Law in Nigeria*, op.cit. P. 29.
[50] Adesanya, S.A, *Law of Matrimonial Causes*, op.cit p.148.
[51] MA s.22.

It should be noted that the Registrar's certificate or the Minister's License is not an evidence of celebration of marriage. They merely indicated that the parties are free from all lawful impediments to celebrate their marriage.

1.1.4.2.3 OBJECTIONS TO MARRIAGE

The essence of the publication of Notice is to inform the public of the intended marriage and to invite anyone who has objections to the intended marriage to raise them before the Registrar issues the Certificate to marry. Any member of the public could raise objections to the marriage by entering the word "FORBIDDEN" opposite the entry of the notice in the Marriage Notice Book and append his name, address, and the ground or grounds for opposing the marriage.[52] When objection is entered, the Registrar should without any delay refer the matter to a Judge of the High Court of a State. The Judge upon the application of the Registrar will summon the parties to the intended marriage and the person who is opposing the marriage before him. The opposing party is expected to justify the ground or grounds for his objection. The Judge is to determine the case in a summary way but the parties have the right to appeal against the decision of the Judge.[53] If the Judge found that the ground or grounds were not justified, he may remove the opposition by canceling the word "FORBIDDEN" in the Marriage Notice Book and write below it "CANCELLED BY ORDER OF HIGH COURT" and signed.[54] He may also award compensation and costs to injured parties if the opposition was entered on insufficient ground or grounds.[55]

---

[52] MA s.14 (1)

[53] MA s.15.

[54] MA s 16.

[55] MA s.17.

It should be noted here that the intended Marriage must take place within three months from the date of the notice to the Marriage Registrar. If not, the notice and all the proceedings consequent thereupon are to be considered void; and fresh notice shall be given before the parties can lawfully marry.[56]. But in computing the time period of three months in relation to the notice where objection was entered, the time that elapsed between the entering of the opposition and its removal is not to be taken into consideration.[57]

1.1.4.3   THE PLACES OF CELEBRATION AND THE ACTUAL STATUTORY FORM TO BE OBSERVED.

When the parties to the intended marriage have obtained the Registrar's Certificate or the Minister's License, they shall then proceed for the celebration of their marriage either:

(1) At the Registrar's Office;
(2) Or a Licensed place of worship
(3) Or the place named in the Minister's License.

1.1.4.3.1   CELEBRATION AT THE REGISTRAR'S OFFICE

The celebration of marriage at the Registrar's Office must be done in line with the following conditions laid down in the Marriage Act[58].

(1) The marriage must be performed before the Registrar of Marriage (who could be regarded as the official witness) and two other persons (who could be seen as common witnesses).
(2) The doors and windows of the Registrar's Office must be kept open throughout the period of the celebration.

---

[56] MA s.12.

[57] MA s. 16.

[58] MA s. 27.

(3) The marriage celebration must take place between the hours of 10.00 and 16.00.

The Marriage must also be celebrated in accordance with the prescribed formula laid down by the Marriage Act. After the Registrar has received the Marriage Certificate or the Minister's License, he is to address the parties either directly or through an interpreter in the following words:

"Do I understand that you, AB and you, CD, come here for the purpose of becoming man and wife?"[59] If the parties answer in the affirmative, he shall make the following explanation or admonition. "Know ye that, by the public taking of each other as man and wife in my presence and in the presence of the persons now here, and by the subsequent attestation thereof by signing your names to that effect, you become legally married to each other, although no other rite of a civil or religious nature shall take place, and that this marriage cannot be dissolved during your life time, except by a valid judgment of divorce; and if either of you before the death of the other shall contract another marriage while this remain un dissolved you will be thereby guilty of bigamy, and liable to punishment for that offence"[60]

After the Registrar's explanation and if the parties still wish to go ahead with the marriage, each of them shall pronounce himself or herself legally married with these prescribed words: "I call upon all persons here present to witness that I, AB., do take thee, CD, to be my lawful wife (or husband)"[61].

With the above words addressed to themselves by the parties in the presence of the witnesses, the celebration comes to an end. At the end

---

[59] MA s. 27.
[60] Ibid.
[61] Ibid.

of the celebration, the parties, their witnesses, and the Registrar of Marriage sign the Marriage Certificate[62] in duplicate. One copy of the Certificate is given to the parties and the Registrar of Marriage files the other in his office.[63]

1.1.4.3.2 CELEBRATION AT A LICENCED PLACE OF WORSHIP

Apart from the Registrar's office, marriage may be celebrated in a licensed place of worship. The Act provides: "Marriage may be celebrated in any licensed place of worship by any recognized minister of the Church, denomination to which such place of worship belongs, and according to the rites or usages of marriage observed in such Church, denomination or body"[64]

Following the above provisions of the Marriage Act, a recognized minister of one religious group cannot officiate at a marriage in a place of worship not licensed for his religious group. Thus a Catholic Priest or deacon cannot officiate at a marriage in a licensed Anglican Place of worship either in accordance with the rites and usages of the Catholic Church or those of the Anglican Communion.

The Minister of religion is not to officiate at a marriage in a licensed place of worship unless the parties deliver to him the Registrar's Certificate or the Minister's License[65]. He is in addition forbidden to officiate at any marriage if he knows of any just impediment.[66] Further, a minister of religion shall not celebrate any marriage except

---

[62] The prescribed Form for the marriage certificate is Form E, first schedule to appendix, See MA s. 25.

[63] MA s.28.

[64] MA s. 21.

[65] MA s 22.

[66] Ibid.

in a building, which has been duly licensed by the Minister, or in the license issued by the Minister.[67]

In addition to the above, the Minister of Religion is not under any obligation to officiate at any marriage brought before him. He has the liberty to accept or refuse to preside at any marriage. The Matrimonial Causes Act made it clear that "a minister of religion shall not be bound to solemnize the marriage of a person whose former marriage has been dissolved, whether in Nigeria or elsewhere, otherwise than by death."[68] In this light, a catholic priest or deacon is not under any duty to celebrate a marriage of one divorced in the civil court without having obtained a decree of nullity from a competent Ecclesiastical Marriage Tribunal.

The celebration at the licensed place of worship must conform to the following conditions:[69]

(1) The doors and windows of the place of worship must be kept open throughout the period of the celebration.
(2) The time for the celebration must be between 8.00 and 18.00.
(3) The celebration must be in the presence of the officiating minister of religion and two or more witnesses.

It should be noted that every religious group or body has its own rites and usages of marriage. However, a common element runs in all marriage celebrations in a licensed place of worship. This common element consists in the declaration by the parties before the recognized minister of religion and the witnesses that they take each other as husband and wife until parted by death.

---

[67]   MA s. 23.
[68]   MCA s. 107.
[69]   MA s.21.

According to Wiles J, other features such as the joining of hands and the giving of rings are mere indications of the marriage, which has already taken place by the exchange of consent of the parties.[70]

Once the celebration is over, the officiating minister of religion "shall fill up in duplicate a marriage certificate with the particulars required by Form E, and state also and enter in the counterfoil, the number of the certificate, the date of the marriage, names of the parties, and the names of the witnesses."[71]

The officiating minister, the parties, and two or more witnesses, shall then sign the Marriage certificate in duplicate. The officiating minister shall sign his name on the counterfoil to the marriage certificate. He shall after signing, severe the duplicate from the counterfoil and shall deliver one certificate to the parties, and shall within seven days thereafter transmit the other to the registrar of marriage for the district in which the marriage took place, who shall file the same in his office.[72]

It is worthy of note that the Principal Registrar has the duty to provide the registrars of marriage and the recognized ministers of religion with books of marriage certificate in duplicate and with counterfoils as in 'Form E'. The several registrars and the ministers of religion keep the books in their custody under lock and key. They are to return the book of marriage certificates, with their counterfoil duly filled in, to the principal registrar, as soon as the certificates contained therein are used up.[73]

---

[70]   Wiles J. in the case of *Beamish v Beamish*, H.L., 9 (1959-1961), p.330.
[71]   MA s. 25.
[72]   MA s. 26.
[73]   MA s. 24.

1.1.4.3.3 CELEBRATION AT A PLACE NAMED IN THE MINISTER'S LICENCE

The minister's license may authorize the celebration of marriage at a place other than a licensed place of worship or the office of the Marriage Registrar.[74] In such a situation, the marriage must be celebrated in the place so named in the license. The officiating minister must be the Registrar of Marriage or the Minister of Religion.[75] The parties with the license will present it to the Registrar of Marriage in the Marriage District of the place where the marriage is to be celebrated. Upon the receipt of the license, the Registrar of Marriage is to issue the parties with a blank certificate of marriage in duplicate. The Minister of Religion or the Registrar who officiated at the celebration shall fill up the blank marriage certificate and observe strictly all the formalities that normally follow marriages done in a licensed place of worship or the registrar's office depending on the case.[76]

1.1.4.3.4 CELEBRATION OUTSIDE NIGERIA

The Marriage Act provides for the situation whereby a Nigerian Citizen living outside Nigeria could celebrate a valid statutory marriage recognized in Nigeria outside Nigeria. This is done in the Nigerian diplomatic missions abroad. For purposes of statutory marriage, Nigerian missions abroad are considered as marriage districts and the Nigerian diplomatic or consular officers of the rank of Secretary and above are seen as Marriage Officers, while their

---

[74] MA s. 13.

[75] MA s. 29; Also see MA s.33 (2) (d), which provides that a marriage shall be null and void if both parties to the marriage knowingly and willfully acquiesce in its celebration by a person who is not a recognized minister of some religious denomination or body, or a registrar of marriage.

[76] MA s.29.

office is considered as Marriage office.[77] Thus marriage of which at least a party is a Nigerian citizen could take place in the Nigerian missions before the Nigerian diplomatic or consular officer of the rank of Secretary or above. The solemnization and the issuance of the Marriage Certificate are as described for marriages at the Registrar's office in Nigeria.

1.1.4.4 OTHER FORMAL NORMS TO BE OBSERVED IN THE CELEBRATION OF MARRIAGE

Both the Marriage Act and the Matrimonial Causes Acts made reference to other formal norms to be observed in the celebration of marriage. These include:

(1) The name or names to be used at the celebration of marriage
(2) Conformity to the law of the place of celebration.

1.1.4.4.1 NAMES TO BE USED FOR MARRIAGE CELEBRAION

For a marriage celebrated under the Act to be valid, the parties to the marriage must use their real correct names; otherwise, the marriage is void.[78] If for instance, the man's real and correct name is AB and the woman's real and correct name is AZ the exchange of consent must be done in those names. It is an offence under the Marriage Act to contract marriage under a false name or names with intent to deceive the other party to the marriage. The punishment for the offence is five years in jail.[79] This requirement of the law is necessary in order to reveal the true identity of the intended couple.

---

[77] MA ss. 50 & 51
[78] MA s 33 (2) (b).
[79] MA s.44.

1.1.4.4.2 CONFORMITY TO THE LAW OF THE PLACE OF CELEBRATION

The Matrimonial Causes Act provides that for a marriage to be valid in Nigeria, it must be celebrated in accordance with the laws of marriage at the place where the marriage was celebrated.[80] In essence, the provisions of the law here is to the effect that when parties to a marriage have fulfilled all the requirements of the law, they must in addition comply with the requirements for the formal celebration of their marriage for it to be valid. Non-compliance with the form therefore renders a marriage null and void. If for example a party contracts marriage in Italy, which does not follow the requirements of form, laid down in Italy for the celebration of marriage, such a marriage will not be recognized in Nigeria. Also if a party contracts marriage other than customary or Islamic marriage in Nigeria without following the provisions of the Marriage Act such marriage will be regarded as null and void in Nigeria. [81] Non-compliance with form renders a marriage null under the Act. Invariable, form is an important issue in the celebration of marriages.

1.1.4.5 PERSONS OBLIGED TO KEEP THE STATUTORY FORM IN NIGERIA

In Nigeria, the statutory form of marriage is meant to be observed by all those who contract statutory marriage. The laws that govern this marriage are the Marriage Act and the Matrimonial Causes Act. These are emanated or deemed to have been given by the National Assembly which is the highest legislative organ in the country.[82]

---

[80] MCA, s.3 (1) (c), This rule comes into effect from the time of the commencement of the MCA. MCA came into effect on March 24, 1971.

[81] MA s.33 (2) (a)-(d).

[82] *The Constitution of the Federal Republic of Nigeria,* 1999, s. 4 (1).

The National Assembly is vested with the constitutional power "to make laws for the peace, order, and good government of the federation or any part thereof with respect to any matter included in the exclusive legislative list set out in part 1 of the second schedule to this constitution."[83]

The National Assembly has the excusive legislative competence to make laws on matters listed in the exclusive legislative list. Item 61 of the exclusive legislative list provides for "the formation, annulment and dissolution of marriages other than marriages under Islamic law and customary law including matrimonial causes relating thereto."[84]

The implication of this constitutional provision is that the National Assembly makes laws that govern marriages in Nigeria apart from those marriages contracted under the Islamic law or the customary law. The statutory form of marriage is therefore meant to be observed by all Nigerians who wish to celebrate marriage in any other way apart from the Islamic law or customary law. All Catholics are therefore bound to observe the statutory norm for the celebration of their marriage to have legal effect in Nigeria.

---

[83] Ibid. s. 4(2).

[84] The *Constitution of the Federal Republic of Nigeria,* 1999, Second Schedule, Part 1, Exclusive Legislative List, item 61 (The previous constitutions of Nigeria have similar provision). By this provision, Moslem marriage is clearly not regulated by the law of the Federal Government on marriage. Moslems are thus free to celebrate their marriage according to their Moslem religious law. One wonders why other religious laws in Nigeria like the canon law for the Catholics should not equally be allowed to govern the marriage of Catholics. Why should one religion be given preference over the other in a country that provides for the freedom of religion and equal treatment of religious sects under the law.?

1.1.4.6 REGISTRATIONS AND EVIDENCE OF MARRIAGE

Every Registrar is required to register all marriage certificates filled in his office in a Marriage Register book according to 'Form F'. Such registrations shall be made in a chronological order and duly signed and authenticated by the registrar himself. This Marriage Register book in 'Form F' shall be so indexed as to allow for easy reference to it.[85] The Registrar shall allow searches to be made in the Marriage Register book and shall give certified copies from it on request, upon payment of the prescribed fee.[86] Within ten days after the last day of each month, every Registrar shall send to the Principal Registrar a certified copy of all entries made by him during the preceding month in the Marriage Register Book of his district, and the Principal Registrar shall file the same in his office.[87] Any registrar could effect a correction of any clerical error in any certificate of marriage filed in his office. To do this, he must be authorized by the Principal Registrar and produce the certificate delivered to the parties. He shall then authenticate every correction by his signature and the date of such correction.[88]

Every certificate of marriage filed in the office of the Registrar of marriage of any district or a copy of it, signed and certified by the registrar of the district, and every entry in the Marriage Register Book or a copy of it, shall be admissible as evidence of the marriage to which it relates in any court of justice or before any person having by law or consent of the parties authority to hear, receive, and examine evidence.[89] The Matrimonial Causes Act empowers the High Courts of States or Federal Capital Territory to "receive as evidence of the facts stated in it a document purporting to be either the original or

---

[85] MA s.30 (1).

[86] MA s.30 (2).

[87] MA s. 30 (3).

[88] MA s.31.

[89] MA s.32.

a certified copy of any certificate, entry or record of a birth, death or marriage alleged to have taken place whether in Nigeria or elsewhere.[90] The Marriage Certificate is thus a vital document in proving the celebration of a statutory marriage either in Nigeria or in a Nigerian diplomatic mission abroad. Parties should therefore make sure that their marriage certificates are duly filed with the registrar of the district where the marriage was celebrated. They should also keep good custody of the duplicate of the Marriage Certificate issued to them on the occasion of the celebration of their marriage.

1.1.5 JUDICIAL PROCESSES DUE TO LACK OR DEFECT OF FORM

A lack of form case occurs in a situation where the required form is absent. For example, the failure of the parties to a marriage to produce the Registrar's Certificate or the Minister's License before the celebration of the marriage. This is different from defect of form cases. In a defect of form case, the form was present but defective in some manner. Conversely, in a lack of form case, the form was never present. Such a designation infers a complete lack of statutory form during the celebration of the marriage.

The law that deals with matrimonial proceedings in Nigeria is "the Marriage Act," "the Matrimonial Causes Act" and "the Matrimonial Causes Rules 1983" made pursuant to "the Matrimonial Causes Act."

The Jurisdiction over Matrimonial Causes is vested on the State High Court.[91] As stated earlier, "the Matrimonial Causes Act" applies only to monogamous marriages celebrated under the Marriage Act.

---

[90]   MCA s. 86.
[91]   MCA, s.2.

The basis for the assumption of Court Jurisdiction over marriage in Nigeria is domicile.[92] Domicile is seen here to mean a person's permanent home. Although Nigeria is a Federation of many states, there is only one single Nigerian domicile for the purpose of jurisdiction under the Matrimonial Causes. Thus once a person is domiciled in any State in Nigeria, he may institute proceedings in any State High Court whether or not he is resident in that State or not.[93]

There are many relieves that may be applied for under the Matrimonial Causes. Among them is the Nullity of void marriage. Under "the Matrimonial Causes Act," a marriage is void under several conditions among which are if the marriage did not conform to the law of the place of celebration by reason of failure to comply with the requirements of the law of that place with respect to the form of solemnization of marriages.[94] Also the Marriage Act[95] provides that "a marriage shall be null and void if both parties knowingly and willfully acquiesce in the celebration of a marriage in:

(a) A place other than the office of a registrar of marriages or a licensed place of worship; or

(b) Under a false name; or

(c) Without a registrar's certificate of notice or license issued under section 13 of this Act duly issued; or

(d) By a person not being a recognized minister of some religious denomination or a registrar of marriage.

---

[92] The court in Nigeria made this clear in the case of *Bhojwani v Bhojwani* reported in NWLR, 6 (1996), pt.457.

[93] In the case of *Adegoroye v Adegoroye*, reported in NWLR, 4 (1996), pt. 472 the court stated also that though there is no express provision relating to transfer of petition from one High Court to another, such power can be inferred since the entire country constitutes one jurisdiction.

[94] MCA, s. 3 (1) (c).

[95] MCA s 33 (2) (a)-(d).

Where a marriage is void, the petitioner may bring a petition for nullity of marriage.[96] A petition for a decree of nullity of marriage shall be in accordance with Form 6.[97] A decree for the nullity of marriage shall, in the first instance, be a decree nisi.[98] A decree nisi becomes absolute after 3 months subject to sections 57 and 58 of the Matrimonial Causes Act.[99] There is no right of appeal against a decree absolute in matrimonial proceedings.[100]

The Nigerian Courts have been called upon on several occasions to determine the nullity of marriage based on section 33 (2) of the Marriage Act. The most frequent cases centre on the lack of the registrar's certificate or the minister's license.

In *Obiekwe v Obiekwe*[101] the court was called upon to determine the validity of a marriage celebrated at the Holy Ghost Roman Catholic Church Enugu, on 30 December 1961, without the parties thereto complying with the provisions of the Marriage Act.

The court held through Palmer J. thus: "A great deal has been said about 'church marriage' or 'Marriage under Roman Catholic Law'. So far as the law of Nigeria is concerned, there is only one form of monogamous marriage, and that is marriage under the Ordinance (Act). Legally a marriage in the Church (or any denomination) is either a marriage under the Ordinance (Act) or it is nothing. In this case, if the parties had not been validly married under the Ordinance

---

[96] MCA s.34.
[97] Matrimonial Causes Rules 1983, Order 5, Rule 18, in *Laws of the Federation of Nigeria, 1990,* cap. 220.
[98] MCA, s.58.
[99] See also the case of *Dejonwo v Dejonwo* reported in NWLR, (1993), Pt. 306.
[100] See also the case of *Towoyemi v Towoyemi* reported in NWLR, (2001), Pt. 702.
[101] ENLR, 7 (1963), pt.196.

(Act) then either they are married under native law or custom or they are not married at all. In either case the ceremony in Church would have made not a scrap of difference to their legal status."

The above stand of the law in Nigeria with regard to non-compliance with the requirements of the Marriage Act was stressed again in the case of *Anyaegbunam v Anyaegbunam*[102] Here the parties were married in a Roman Catholic Church in Abatete on 28th January 1961. In 1971 the wife brought a petition for "judicial separation." The husband claimed that the court has no jurisdiction, as he did not contract a monogamous marriage with the wife but a customary marriage followed by Church blessing or wedding. The trial court ruled that the husband intended a monogamous marriage. On appeal the Supreme Court, which is the highest court in Nigeria, ruled that the trial court has no jurisdiction. Affirming that the marriage since it did not comply with the provisions of the Marriage Act is not a statutory marriage to be handled by the civil courts. According to the court, what happened in the Church was a mere blessing of a customary marriage.

However before considering a marriage null and void for non compliance with the provisions of the *Marriage Act* or as a mere blessing of the customary marriage as we have seen in the above cases the element of willfulness and knowledge on the side of both parties should be considered.

In *Akuwudike v Akuwudike* [103] the court was invited to determine the validity of a marriage entered by the parties at St. Mary's Catholic Church Port Harcourt in the presence of a Roman Catholic Priest and two witnesses. The Registrar's certificate was not produced, as the parties did not enter any notice of marriage. Neither did they obtain the Minister's license. The Marriage was simply celebrated without

---

[102] S.C., 4 (1973), pt.121
[103] ENLR, 7 (1963), pt.56.

compliance with the requirement of the Marriage Act. The wife petitioned for divorce. It was argued on behalf of the respondent that the Court lacks jurisdiction, as there was no marriage under the Act. It was also further argued that the marriage was void because there was no Registrar's certificate. It was however found to be the fact that the petitioner has no knowledge of the legal requirements of a valid marriage under the Act. Moreover it was her intention that she was going through a marriage recognized by the Church as well as the Law of Nigeria. The issue of knowledge and willfully acquiescing was ruled out in relation to her. The Court through Idigbe J. (as he then was) held: ". . . if it is the intention of the parties to get married under the Ordinance (Act) and they believed that they went through a form of marriage recognized by law, i.e., the Ordinance, then if the marriage had been performed by a Minister of Religion in a place of worship licensed under the Ordinance for the purpose, the marriage in my view would not be void merely by reason of non-compliance with sections 11 and 13 unless it was affirmatively shown that parties (both parties) willfully and knowingly failed to comply with the said sections."

A similar position was taken in *Akparanta v Akparanta*[104] Here a marriage celebrated in the Roman Catholic Church without the Registrar's certificate or the Minister's license was held to be valid for the above reason that both parties to the marriage could not be held to have knowingly and willfully failed to comply with the provisions of the Marriage Act.

Be that as it may, ignorance of the law may not always be an excuse. The position of the law in Nigeria today is that for a person to contract a valid marriage apart from the customary law marriage or the Islamic Law marriage, the parties must conform to the provision of the Marriage Act with regard to the formal celebration of marriage. Otherwise, the marriage will be declared null and void and of no legal consequence.

---

[104] ECSLR, 2 (1972), pt. 779.

SECTION TWO
THE CUSTOMARY FORM IN NIGERIA

1.2.1 MEANING AND NATURE OF THE NIGERIA CUSTOMARY LAW

The term customary law in the Nigeria context is used to refer to the customs that have been accepted as binding among members of an ethnic community. There are two kinds of customary law operative in Nigeria. The first is the indigenous customs that are considered binding in the various ethnic communities that constitute the federation of Nigeria. The second is the Moslem law, often called the Shari a law which is a religious law that binds among those who profess the religion of Islam. This is not indigenous to any ethnic community in Nigeria. It was introduced among some ethnic tribes in the Northern part of Nigeria as a result of conversion to the religion of Islam.

The ethnic community customary law in Nigeria has the following basic features:

First, they are generally unwritten.[105] The reason for this is not far fetched. The indigenous ethnic communities in Nigeria at the beginning[106] are illiterate communities. The laws which they considered binding and with which they regulate their social life was therefore unwritten. However, with western education and civilization, there is effort to put most of these laws in writing and to read written documents in the light of customary law.[107].

---

[105] Obilade, A.O., *the Nigerian Legal System*, (Ibadan: Spectrum Books Ltd, 2001), p. 64.

[106] At the beginning here we mean before the phenomenon of colonization and the subsequent western civilization and education that followed.

[107] *Alfa v. Arepo*, WNLR, (1963), 95; *Rotibi v. Savage* NLR, 17 (1944),77.

A second feature of the ethnic community customary law in Nigeria is its diversity. Nigeria is a multi-ethnic nation. There are over two hundred and fifty different ethnic groups in Nigeria. Each of this group has their specific customs. Even among the same ethnic group these customs may vary from one group of the same ethnic community to another group of that same ethnic community. This fact of diversity in the ethnic customary law in Nigeria has made it almost impossible to have a uniform system of customary law that could be operative in the whole of Nigeria.

Acceptability is another feature of ethnic community customary law. The customs in question must be accepted by the members of the ethnic group as binding among them. A norm cannot be seen as binding if the people the norm is meant for refused to accept it as binding. Ethnic customary laws therefore are those laws which the members of the ethnic group accept and consider as binding among them.[108]

Lastly, the ethnic customary law in Nigeria is flexible. Indeed, flexibility is a notorious feature of ethnic customary law in Nigeria. It changes as the people changes. It is always in tune with the changing circumstances due to economic and socio-political variations. Flexibility in ethnic customary law is noted by the court in the case of *Lewis v Bankole*[109] thus: "One of the most striking features of West African native custom . . . is its flexibility; it appears to have been always subject to motives of expediency, and it shows unquestionable adaptability to altered circumstances without entirely losing its character."

---

[108] See *Owonyin v Omotosho*, ALL NLR, (1961), 304, where the court described ethnic customary law as "a mirror of accepted usage." Also see *Eshugbayi Eleko v. Government of Nigeria*, AC, (1931), pt. 662 at p. 673 where the court stated that an obligatory customary law must be accepted by the members of the ethnic community.

[109] NLR 1 (1908), pt. 81 at pp. 100-101.

The flexibility of the ethnic customary law could be understood from the back drop of the introduced western civilization. If the custom has to be accepted, it must be able to adapt itself to the sociological realities of the time. On account of the flexibility of the ethnic customary laws, it is very difficult in some cases to ascertain them with certainty.

The ethnic customary law accepted in Nigeria must not contradict any written law in force in Nigeria. Also ethnic customary laws that are contrary to natural justice, equity and good conscience or that is manifestly obnoxious are not regarded as valid customary laws in Nigeria.[110]

Unlike the ethnic customary law, the Moslem law is generally written and is not amenable to changes. They are based on the Koran, the practice of the prophet, the consensus opinion of scholars, and the analogical deductions from the Koran and the practice of the prophet.[111] In Nigeria, the version of the Moslem law in practice is the *Maliki* School.

The Moslem law is classified among the customary laws in Nigeria. For us, there is no basis for this classification. It is very clear that Moslem law is not indigenous to any ethnic community that constitute the present day Nigeria. Moslem law is a received law which came about with the conversion of some tribes in the Northern and West Southern part of Nigeria into the religion of Islam. It is our view that the classification of Moslem law as customary law in Nigeria is wrong. This work will therefore not delve into the treatment of the form of marriage in Moslem law as part of the customary practices

---

[110] See *Supreme Court Ordinance*, 1876, s. 19, which empower courts to apply "native law or custom" not "repugnant to natural justice, equity and good conscience."

[111] Obilade, op. cit., p. 83.

in Nigeria. The constitution of Nigeria clearly shows that Islamic marriage is different from the customary marriage.[112].The Moslem law is a religious law that governs the religious life of the adherents of the Muslim religion in Nigeria just as the canon law regulates the life of Catholic faithful in Nigeria. One might question here why is it that the Muslim law which is purely religious is allowed under the constitution of the Federal republic of Nigeria to govern the marriage of the Muslims in Nigeria whereas canon law, an equally religious law is not recognized by the same constitution to govern the marriage of Catholics? This is part of the unfair treatment of the Catholic law and we should be postulating in the subsequent pages for its recognition like the Muslim law in Nigeria in the area of marriage and Catholics personal life.

1.2.2 THE NATURE OF MARRIAGE UNDER NIGERIA CUSTOMARY LAWS

Even though customary laws in Nigeria vary from one ethnic community to the other, the nature of marriage under the customary laws are basically the same. Marriage under the customary laws is potentially polygamous.

By polygamy here is meant "polygyny." This is "the condition or practice of having more than one wife."[113] This is the practice among the indigenous communities in Nigeria. There are several reasons that could account for this practice.

---

[112] See the *Constitution of the Federal Republic of Nigeria 1999,* Second Schedule, part 1, exclusive legislative list, item 61 (previous constitutions, namely the 1954, 1963 and the 1979 constitutions have similar provisions) which excludes Islamic marriage distinct from customary marriage from the exclusive legislative list of the Federal Government.

[113] Garner, B:A et al. (eds), *Blacks Law dictionary,* op.cit., p. 1180.

First and foremost is the desire of people to have as many children as possible. Children are seen as the pride of parent. People tend to have more than one wife in order to have as many children as possible.

Further, childless marriage gives room to having more than one wife. There is also the quest to have male issues who will inherit the parent. Female issues are not subject of inheritance under the native laws and customs in Nigeria. So people, who do not have male issues in their marriage, tend to get more wives in order to have male offspring.

Further still, many tend to marry more wives for economic reasons. The more wives, the more children and invariable the more hand to till the soil and produce income.

The opposite practice which is "polyandry" that is "the condition or practice of having more than one husband"[114] is never the case in Nigeria. In the case of *Kpelanya v Tsoka and Anors*[115] the court in Nigeria held that under Tiv customary law a woman could not lawfully be married to two men at the same time. It is an offence under some customary laws in Nigeria for a woman to have more than one husband concurrently.[116]

The non acceptance of "polyandry" by the customary laws in Nigeria is a good practice and quite commendable. A woman should not have more than one husband at the same time. "Polygyny" should therefore not be encouraged. A man should not have more than one wife at the same time. This is because in the original divine plan of marriage, God made it between one man and one woman. Not one man and two or more women, nor one woman and two or more men. When

---

[114] *Black's Law dictionary*, op.cit., p.1180.
[115] NNLR, (1971), 86.
[116] See for example, *the Native Authority (Declaration of Idoma Native Marriage law and custom) Order*, 1959, s. 6(2).

marriage is between a man and a woman, the dignity of both will be respected. The quest for the male issue which we gave above as part of the reason for many men marrying more than one wife will be dropped if both men and women under the customary law are given equal dignity and status. The male child is not of more value than the female child.

1.2.3   PRELIMINARIES TO CUSTOMARY LAW MARRIAGE

Before marriage under customary law in Nigeria takes place, the parties concerned must make their intention to marry known to their respective families. The families and the parties themselves will then carry out extensive enquiries to determine the suitability of the parties to marry each other.

There is no laid down format for carrying out this investigation. The goal of the enquiry however is to uncover anything that would be an obstacle or bar to the proposed marriage such as social status, hereditary illness, bad character traits, bonds of consanguinity and affinity, maturity and responsibility in general etc.

Once these enquiries are over and the families and the parties are satisfied as to their suitability to marry, a formal announcement of the intention to enter into marriage will be made with the ceremony of "betrothal."[117] This is a prelude to the intended marriage celebration.

---

[117] For detailed discussion on the ceremony of betrothal see Onokah M.C. *Familiy law,* (Ibadan: Spectrum books limited, 2003) pp. 72-74; Nwogugu, E.I., *Family law in Nigeria,* (Ibadan: Heinemann Education books, 1974) p.20-21; Obi, S.N.C., *The Customary Law Manual,* (Enugu: Government press, 1977), pp. 25-226.

1.2.4. THE CELEBRATION OF MARRIAGE UNDER CUSTOMARY LAW

Marriage celebration under customary law has three main features.[118]

1. The public manifestation of consent by the parties
2. The giving and the acceptance of the "marriage token" (dowry)
3. The formal handing over of the bride to the groom

1.2.4.1 THE PUBLIC MANIFESTATION OF CONSENT

Consent is an essential requirement of marriage under the customary law. There can be no marriage without consent. In the main, there are two types of consent required under the customary law. The first is the consent of the parties themselves. The second is the consent of their parents.

The parties to a marriage must come to an agreement that they intend to take each other as man and wife. In a situation where the woman did not consent to marry the man the Supreme Court in Nigeria has ruled that there is no valid customary law marriage.[119]

---

[118] Lewin J., *Studies in African Native Law* (Cape Town: The African Bookman, 1947), p. 35.

[119] See the case of *Osamwonyi v Osamwonyi*, SC, 10 (1972), 1;(*In this case, the petitioner filed for the nullity of a marriage he contracted under the act with the respondent on the ground that the respondent was married to another man under customary law before he contracted the statutory marriage with her. The respondent was able to prove that she did not give her consent for the said customary law marriage to another man. The court ruled that the consent of the bride must be had and obtained before a valid customary law marriage under Benin customary law*).

It is a criminal offence in Nigeria to keep a woman without her wish with the intent to contract marriage with her.[120]

The consent of the parties is publicly expressed during the marriage celebration itself. This usually takes place at the home of the bride during a joint meeting of the two families with their representatives.

It happen like this, the head of the family of the bride will hold a cup filed with wine. He will ask the bride if she consents to the marriage the celebration of which is about taking place. The bride gives her accent by sipping from the cup of wine.[121] She will then be asked to present the cup of wine to the groom if he is present or to the representative of the groom. If the groom or his representative sips from the cup of wine as well, he shows that he consented to the marriage. This simple act of the bride and the groom to wit sipping from the same cup in the presence of their family members and representatives shows their consent to marry each other as man and wife.

The consent of the parents of the groom and the bride are also vital in customary law marriage. This is indicated by the fact that marriage under customary law has to take place at the home of the bride and in the presence of the family members of the groom and the bride.

The consent of the bride's parent is particularly very necessary. The father of the bride or the person acting in his place must have to accent to the marriage. His accent is important because of the role he has to play on the occasion of the marriage celebration itself. For instance, as we have seen above, he is the one who presents the bride

---

[120] "Criminal Code" op. cit., s.361. (This states *"Any person who, with the intent to marry . . . a female person of any age, or to cause her to be married . . . by any other person, takes her away, or detains her against her will, is guilty of a felony and is liable to imprisonment for seven years"*).

[121] Kasumu, A.B, Salacuse, J.W., *Nigeria Family Law,*(London: Butterworths, 1966), p. 75.

with the cup of wine from which she sips and gives to her groom. In our later discussion, he is the one who will accept the "dowry" and perform the ceremony of formal handing over of the bride to the groom. He can be identified as the key witness in the marriage celebration. One may equate him as the official witness of the family in the marriage celebration.

In the case of *Adisatu Awero v Olajida Ishola*,[122] the court held that customary marriage without the consent of the girl's parent is invalid. In the same vein, the High court of Benue State of Nigeria in the case of *Dura Aonde v Yomekaa Agoii*[123] declared that "no marriage is valid under the Tiv customary law unless the father or the person acting in *loco parentis* consents."

The right of women under the customary law is not very pronounced. The consent of the mother of the girl to the marriage though necessary is not essential to the validity of the customary law marriage. In *Obasi & Ors v Obasi*[124] the court ruled that if the mother did not give her consent and as such refuses to participate in the customary marriage celebration, that the subsequent customary marriage cannot be invalidated.

Parental consent however cannot under any condition be unreasonable withheld. If this be the case, the law in many cases provides a remedy. For example, section 5 of *Marriage, Divorce and Custody of Children Adoptive Bye-Laws Order* 1958, promulgated by the Western Region government, states: "When any parent or guardian of a bride refuses his or her consent to a marriage or refuses to accept his or her own share of the dowry, the bride, if she is eighteen years of age or above,

---

[122] (1962), Case no. B/229/62, Grade 'B', C.C., Egba Odeda; this case was reported in Obi, S.N.C., *Modern Family Law in Southern Nigeria*, (London: Sweet & Maxwell, 1966) pp. 161-162.

[123] Suit no. GBB/32A/1981, (unreported).

[124] ISLR, (1979), p. 558.

and the bridegroom jointly may institute legal proceedings in a competent court against the parent or guardian to show cause why he or she should refuse consent or to accept his or her share of the dowry; and if the court is of the opinion that no sufficient cause has been shown, it shall order that the marriage may proceed without the consent of such parent"

The above statement of the law is an indication that under customary law, parental consent may not be withheld unreasonably. When that becomes the case, a petition could be made to the court who will grant a waiver.

1.2.4.2 THE GIVING AND THE ACCEPTING OF THE "MARRIAGE TOKEN"[125]

The Celebration of customary law marriage in Nigeria is full of signs and symbols. These have their customary connotations. As we have seen above, to ask and receive the consent of the bride and the groom, the bride is presented with a cup filled with wine from which she drinks and hands over to the groom to drink. The mere sipping from the same cup tells volumes that they are willing to live as man and wife without uttering any word. This is a fantastic gesture.

For the bride's family to show that they have indeed welcome the proposal of the groom to be the husband of their daughter, the groom has to present the family of the bride a "token" which is tied to the marriage. The acceptance of the "token" symbolizes the acceptance of the marriage. The rejection of the "token" shows the rejection of the

---

[125] By "marriage token" We mean something money or money worth agreed upon by the families of the parties to a customary law marriage and presented by the grooms family to the bride's family upon acceptance of which by the bride's family the marriage is sealed.

marriage. Likewise, the return of the "token" indicates the end of the marriage.

This marriage "token," on which the marriage is tied, has been described by many authors as "dowry"[126], "bride-price"[127], or "marriage symbol."[128] No matter the name it is called, it should be remembered that customary indigenous language in Nigeria is not the English language. Sometimes, translating some acts in the culture into the English language cannot but lead to confusion of language. Suffice it to say that under the customary law, there is particular item be it a certain sum of money or otherwise which is given and received in the name of the customary marriage. It symbolizes as it were the life of the marriage. We call this in this work "the marriage token."

Who gives this marriage token? Who receives the marriage token? When and how is the marriage token given?

---

[126] The "dowry" is the "dos" under the Roman law. In the strict sense, it is used to refer to the property which the woman brings to her husbands house—See Corbett, P.E., *The Roman Law of Marriage,* op. cit., p. 147. Because of this original meaning, it is argued by some authors that it does not described what is given and accepted under the customary law—see Onokah, M.C., *Family Law,* (Ibadan: Spectrum books Ltd., 2003), pp. 98-101.

[127] The "bride price" is ". . . any gift or payment, in money, natural produce, brace rods, cowries or in any other kind of property whatsoever, to a parent or guardian of a female person on account of a marriage of that person which is intended or has taken place"—See "Limitation of Dowry Law," in *Laws of Eastern Nigeria,* 1963, cap. 76, s.2; Also see *the Marriage, Divorce and Custody of Children Adoptive By-Laws, Order, 1958* s.2, which defines "bride.price" as" a customary gift made by a husband to or in respect of a woman at or before marriage." For some authors the idea of "bride-price" indicates a sale of the woman to the man.

[128] Onokah, M.C., *Family Law,* op. cit., pp. 90-101 used the term "marriage symbol" in place of the term "bride price."

The marriage token is given by the groom's family to the bride's family. The member of the bride's family who normally receives the marriage token is the father of the bride or his male representative.

In the judicial case of *Okeke v Okeke & ors*[129] the high court in Onitsha in the then East Central State of Nigeria ruled that in the absence of the father, the eldest male son of the family should receive the marriage token of a daughter of the family entering into marriage. This is an indication that under the customary law in Nigeria, the giving and receiving of the marriage token must be properly done in accordance with the custom of the people.

The marriage token is normally negotiated and given on the occasion of the marriage celebration. Elders or representatives of the two families normally go to an inner room for this negotiation. The negotiation is done by the use of broom sticks in most part of the Ibo land. It does not normally constitute a problem. There is always an agreement as what is being offered is nothing but something on which the marriage is tied.

1.2.4.3 THE FORMAL HANDING OVER OF THE BRIDE TO THE GROOM

This is the culmination of the customary law marriage. It is an essential part of the customary marriage celebration. Without it, the marriage is not complete.

On this matter, T.O. Elias remarked "It is the formal handing over of the girl to her husband that really completes the marriage."[130]

---

[129] (1966), Suit no. O/26N1965 of 28/3/66 (unreported), Onitsha High Court.

[130] Elias, T.O., *Groundwork of Nigeria Law,* (London: Routledge & Kegan Paul, 1954), p. 283.

This legal opinion of T.O. Elias was judicially baptized in the case of *Ikedingwu v Okafor*[131] where the court ruled that marriage under the customary law is not complete "until the girl according to custom is taken to the house of the man."

The manner this handing over of the bride to the groom is done varies from one culture to the other. In some cultures, it takes place at the house of the bride, while in others at the house of the groom.

It is to be noted that before the formal handing over of the bride to the groom, the parties must have publicly manifested their consent to be husband and wife. Likewise, the marriage token must have been given and accepted. It is only after these that the grand finale, the formal handing over could validly take place.

The formal handing over of the bride to the groom normally takes place at the end of the marriage feast. The bride may accompany her husband to his house. But usually, the bride is led by some of her girl friends to her husband's house at the end of the marriage feast.

The Customary Law Manual[132] described the manner of handing over of the bride to the groom thus: "the bride in her maiden home is handed over by her father to the marriage middleman who in turn hands her over to the bridegroom in the presence of members of both families. The bride is then taken home by the bridegroom's people."

Whatever method is followed, it is sufficient to state here that customary marriage in Nigeria is brought to an end by the formal

---

[131] ENLR (1966), p. 178.

[132] *The Customary Law Manual,* op.cit., p. 256; other methods of handing-over of the bride among the Igbos of Nigeria are described in pp. 250-257 of the manual.

handing over of the bride to the groom. This constitutes an essential element in the customary marriage.[133]

1.2.5 REGISTRATION AND PROOF OF CUSTOMARY MARRIAGE

There are no strict rules governing the registration of customary law marriages in Nigeria. Reliance is often placed on the fact that the celebration of marriage under customary law is clouded by public celebration. It always involves the families of the groom and the bride. The man cannot just pick the woman and they begin to live as husband and wife. Their families are involved.

This publicity notwithstanding, there is a limit to which reliance can be based on people's memory. There is the need to have some sort of record of the event or ceremony that has taken place. This is very nice in case the people who witness the marriage are death. There is therefore the effort in various part of the country to have the customary law marriages registered. The local authorities are authorized by the various Local Government By-laws to register customary law marriages within their jurisdiction.[134]

The Registration of Marriages Adoptive Bye-law Order, 1956[135] which applies in the states of Lagos, Ogun, Oyo, Ondo and former Bendel made the registration of customary law marriages compulsory. It requires the husband of a customary law marriage to register the

---

[133] See *Beckley v Abiodun*, NLR, 17 (1943),59 where Ames J. states that "an essential part of a marriage is the giving of the bride to the bridegroom." Also in *Bolatito, A v Albert, B* (1960) (unreported), the Grade B Customary Court in Ilesha stated that failure to perform the handing over ceremony vitiates customary law marriage.

[134] See for example, *Anambra Local Government Law*, 1976, s.6; *Kano Local Government Law*, 1977, s.10.

[135] *WRLN,* no.4 of 1957.

marriage within one month of its celebration. Failure to do this is an offence punishable under the law. The registration is made in the appropriate book of the Local government authority by the marriage register (which is the person appointed by the local government for this purpose). The appropriate marriage register is open to the public. Anybody could make copies of it upon payment of a prescribed fee.

In some Local government areas, non-registration of the customary law marriage within the prescribed time renders the marriage null and void. This was the decision of the court in *Ashiv v. Agbende*[136] where the court finds that the non-compliance with section 2(e) of *the Native Authority (Declaration of Tiv Native Law and Custom) Order*, 1955[137] with regard to the registration of customary law marriage renders the marriage invalid.

It should be noted however that in many local government areas, the registration of customary law marriages is not made compulsory and there is no punishment attached for non-registration.[138] In many others, there are no Bye-laws at all that governs the registration of marriage. The overall result is that it is not all customary law marriages in Nigeria that are registered.

As for the proof of customary law marriages, reliance is laid on the record of registration in those areas where registration of customary law marriages is a law. But in those areas where the registration of customary law marriages is not provided for, strict rule of proof are followed. The customary law of marriage of the area concerned has first to be established. Then the essentials of such marriage showed. Then after, credible witnesses are to testify as to the fact of

---

[136] FNR, 1(1976), 216.

[137] *NRLN*, no.149 of 1955.

[138] See for example, *Anambra Local Government Law*, 1976, s.55 (9); Local government Law, *Laws of Lagos State*, 1972, cap.74, s. 71 (32).

the celebration of the marriage. The most credible witnesses are normally those who witness the marriage celebration.[139] However, a non-contested evidence of a party or the parties to the marriage could also be used to establish the fact of the celebration of the customary law marriage.[140]

1.2.6 OTHER TYPES OF CUSTMOARY MARRIAGE IN NIGERIA AND THEIR INCIDENCES.

Under some customary law in Nigeria, there are special types of marriages which normally do not follow the above ceremony of marriage. Such marriages include: the *levirate* marriage, the *sororate* marriage, wife procurement marriage.

The levirate marriage is common in most cultures in Nigeria. Among the Ibos of Eastern Nigeria and the Yoruba's of Western Nigeria this practice is common. At the death of the husband, the wife is free to choose any of the relatives of his late husband or even son of his late husband by another woman for a husband. The court in Nigeria affirmed this practice in *the Estate of Agboruja—Deceased*[141]

In *sororate* marriage, at the demise of the wife, the family of the wife will present the living husband with another member of their family for a wife. In such case, the new wife simply takes the place of the old wife.

---

[139] See *the cases of Lawal v younan*, WNLR *(1959),*155; *Adeyemi v. Bamidele, ALL NLR* (1968),*31, 34; Adepeju v Aderei* WNLR, *(1961)154; Abisogun v Abisogun* ALL NLR, (1963), *237; Shashie v Salako*, NMLR, 1 (1976),160; *Igbokwe v U:C:H: Board of Management,* WNLR, (1961),173.

[140] See *Agongo v Aseleke & ors*, NMLR, (1961),21, where the supreme court of Nigeria held that the uncontradicted evidence of a party to the marriage was sufficient proof to establish the marriage.

[141] NLR, 19 (1949), 38.

In the wife procurement marriage, a barren woman marries another woman in the name of her husband for the purpose of procuring children for the husband. This is sometimes erroneously called "woman to woman" marriage. The court in the case of *J.C. Egwu v. Meribe*[142] affirmed the practice as a custom in some part of Nigeria.

1.2.7 JUDICIAL PROCEEDINGS INVOLVING CUSTOMARY MARRIAGE

There is in Nigeria Customary and Area courts. These are courts established for the administration of customary laws. In the north, they are called Area courts. In the south they are called customary courts. These courts have original jurisdiction "in matrimonial causes and matters between persons married under customary law or arising from or connected with a union contracted under customary law.[143] Appeals lie from the customary courts or Area Courts, in the first instance, to Customary Courts of Appeal, or in the Northern States to the Upper Area Courts. These courts have both original and appellate jurisdiction in all matters relating to matrimonial causes under customary law.

The applicable law in the court is the customs prevailing in the area of the jurisdiction of the court which are not repugnant to natural justice, equity and good conscience and are not incompatible with any written law in force at the time. Customary courts are given mandate in civil matters and matrimonial causes, to promote reconciliation among the parties to the suits before it.[144]

---

[142] SC, 3 (1976), 23.

[143] See for example, Ondo State, Customary *court law,* 1981, s. 17.

[144] Ondo State, *Customary courts law,* 1981, s.19.

This judicial proceedings not withstanding, most issues dealing with customary law marriages are handled in an extrajudicial way by the elders of the families of the parties to the customary law marriage. It is often only when there is a deadlock in agreement among the families of the parties that recourse is had to the customary courts.[145]

---

[145] For more detailed information with regard to the constitution and operation of the customary courts in Nigeria, see p.82f.

CHAPTER TWO

OBSERVATIONS, COMPARISONS, AND PROPOSALS

This chapter is extracted from the chapter four of our entire thesis. We intend here to have an overview of what we have done. We shall discuss the basic reasons why the legal systems namely the canon law system which we discussed extensively in chapter two of our entire work, the statutory law and the customary law establish form for the celebration of marriage. We shall also treat the basic similarities and differences in the above listed forms. The problems encountered on account of the multiplicity of forms in Nigeria will equally be highlighted. Possible solution will be suggested to contain the problems.

2.1 THE GENERAL REASON FOR THE ESTABLISMENT OF FORMAL REQUIREMENT OF MARRIAGE CELEBRATIONS.

The three legal systems discussed above namely, the canonical, the Nigeria statutory and the Nigeria customary law established respectively forms for the celebration of marriage. What is the motivating reason for establishing laws that govern form of celebration of marriage?

Judging from our study so far one could identify the following as reasons for the establishment of the formal requirements for the celebration of marriage:

1. Exercise of power and authority over marriage of subjects
2. Prevention of secret marriages and the evils associated with it
3. Uniformity in marital laws
4. Exposition of marital impediments
5. Instructions for the couples on the rights and obligations of marriage.

2.1.1 EXERCISE OF POWER AND AUTHORITY OVER MARRIAGE OF SUBJECTS

The Church, the State of Nigeria and the customary communities in Nigeria exercise influence over marriage of their subjects. They achieve this by respectively establishing invalidating formal requirements for the celebration of marriage.

The authority of the Church over all the baptized Catholics has never been questioned. The Church claims authority over marriage of Catholics anywhere in the world. Canon 1059 categorically states:

Matrimonium catholicorum, etsi una tantum pars sit catholica, regitur iure non solum divino, sed etiam canonico, salva competentia civilis potestatis circa mere civiles eiusdem matrimonii effectus.

The marriage involving at least one Catholic is governed not only by the divine law but also by canon law with reference to the civil authorities with respect only to merely civil effect of the marriage.

By this canon, the Church claims exclusive right to legislate in marriages affecting at least one Catholic member.[146] This right is proper and integral to the nature of the Church by virtue of its mission in the world. One of the manifestations of the Church's authority over marriage of which at least a party is a Catholic is the introduction of the invalidating canonical form.

Any Catholics therefore who enters into a marriage without observing the canonical form celebrates an invalid marriage. The marriage will be from the beginning null and void in the eyes of the Church. Every Catholic is thus under obligation to observe Church law on marriage if they are to marry validly. By establishing an invalidating canonical form the Church exercises power and authority over her subjects (Catholics).

The state of Nigeria also desires to have control over her citizens. The authority of the State over her subjects is even affirmed by the Church.[147] One of the areas the State exercises this power is in the area of marriage. Thus that marriage purported to be a civil marriage and to have civil effect in Nigeria is declared invalid if it does not conform to the formalities established by the State in the *Marriage Act* and the *Matrimonial Causes Act.*

The customary society in Nigeria is also very powerful over her subjects. Nigeria as we stated above is made up of diverse ethnic nationalities that were knitted together with the amalgamation of the Southern and Northern Protectorate by the British colonial powers in 1914 to form the entity today called Nigeria. Each of the ethnic nationalities that constitute the federation of Nigeria is still very active with its cultures and customs notwithstanding the

---

[146] Goldsmith, J.W., "The competence of Church and State over Marriage—Disputed Points," in *The Jurist,* 6 (1946), pp.195-201.

[147] John XXIII, *Pacem in Terris,* (Encyclical letter of 11 April 1963), in *AAS,* 55 (1963), 257.

civil forms in Nigeria. Thus the Nigeria civil society accords these ethnic nationalities autonomy in the area of marriage that affects them within their respective cultures and customs. Customary laws in Nigeria thus establish invalidating customary formalities for the celebration of customary marriage.

2.1.2 PREVENTION OF SECRET MARRIAGE AND EVILS ASSOCIATED WITH IT

A second reason why the legal systems establish formalities for the celebration of marriage is to prevent secret marriage (marriages that are not recognized in the eyes of the respective societies), and the evil associated with it.

The Church strives from the earliest times to prevent secret marriages.[148] This proved for a long time to be a difficult exercise because of the fact that even though the Church before the decree *Tamesi* of the Council of Trent forbids secret marriages it still recognizes its validity. It is only with the promulgation of the decree *Tamesi* and its subsequent modifications by later legislations of the Church that secret marriages were declared invalid. The invalidating canonical form was therefore invented to nail secret marriages.

It provides for the public celebration, proper witnessing and recording of marriage for the good of the marriage and the society at large.[149]

The statutory formalities and the customary formalities for the celebration of marriage are all geared towards making the celebration of marriage a public celebration. It provides for the celebration of marriage in ways recognizable by all the members of the society. This guarantees the basic essential social nature of marriage.

---

[148] Supra, chapter one, section one.
[149] Abbo, J. A., "The Form of Marriage," in *Priest,* 20 (1964), pp. 64-66.

2.1.3 UNIFORMITY OF MARITAL LAWS

The need to have uniformity in the celebration of marriage is still another reason why the marriage forms were evolved.

It is the wish of the Church to have a uniform norm governing the form of marriage celebration. Since the Church is universal and has subjects all over the world, a uniform law of marriage that governs her members anywhere in the world would be an ideal. This will enhance the unity of the Church. Thus after the flaws in the promulgation of the decree *Tametsi*[150], the decree *Ne-temere*[151] corrected the resulting confusion in making the law on form universal and binding on all Catholics. This uniform form is found in the code of canon law for the Latin Rite and the code of canon law for the Eastern Churches.

Similarly, the codification of the marriage laws in Nigeria in the *Marriage Act* of 1914 and in the *Matrimonial Causes Act* of 1970 is with a view of having a uniform system of marriage celebration operative in the whole of Nigeria. There is therefore in Nigeria no other way of celebrating a statutory marriage without following the provision of these Acts. The Acts provides a uniform procedure for the celebration of statutory marriage in Nigeria.

There is equally a relative uniformity in the essential elements involved in the formal celebration of a customary law marriage.[152] Among a given cultural group or tribe in Nigeria marriages are celebrated by following a particular procedure common in the area.

---

[150] Supra, chapter one, section two.

[151] Ibid.

[152] Oyewo, A.T.A., *Handbook on African Laws on Marriages, Inheritance, and Succession Jator,* 1999, pp.21,24; also see supra, chapter three, section two.

2.1.4 **EXPOSITION OF MARITAL IMPEDIMENTS**

Marital impediments are the legal obstacles to contracting a valid marriage.[153]

The Church law stipulated matrimonial impediments.[154] The presence of any of them is a bar to marriage. These impediments can be exposed by means of applying the Church's law on the form for the celebration of marriage.

During the preliminary enquires before the actual celebration of marriage most of these impediments could be brought to light where they exist. The dispensation from these impediments where the law allows it can be granted only by an ordained minister (the priest or the bishop).

The parish priest thus has the duty to explain the impediments and dispense when possible.[155] This is one of the basic reasons why an official witness of the Church was demanded for marriage celebrations. Without the parties to the marriage first appearing before their parish priest most of these impediments might not be discovered.

The state of Nigeria also established marital impediments in the statutory law books.[156] The whole process of obtaining the Registrar's

---

[153] *Blacks Law dictionary,* op. cit., p. 753.

[154] *CIC,* 1983, cc. 1083-1094.

[155] Woywod, "Obligation of Pastor to Examine and Instruct Parties Before Marriage," in *The Homiletic and Pastoral Review,* 37 (1937), pp. 744-745.

[156] MA s. 33 which states "(1), No marriage in Nigeria shall be valid where either of the parties thereto at the time of the celebration of such marriage is married under customary law to any person other than the person with whom such marriage is had. (2) A marriage shall

Certificate to marry or the Minister's License which is part of the formal requirements for the celebration of the statutory marriage in Nigeria is to expose any impediment to marriage. Without the Registrar's certificate or the Minister's license which states that the parties are free to marriage, a valid statutory marriage may not take place in Nigeria.

The customary laws also have matrimonial impediments.[157] Under the customary law in Nigeria, preliminary investigation must precede

---

be null and void if both parties knowingly and willfully acquiesce in its celebration—(a) in any place other than the office of a registrar of marriages or a licensed place of worship (except where authorized by license issued under section 13 of this Act); or (b) under a false name or names; or (c) without a registrar's certificate of notice or license issued under section 13 of this Act duly issued; or (d) by a person not being a recognized minister of some religious denomination or body or a registrar of marriages. (3) But no marriage shall, after celebration, be deemed invalid by reason that any provision of this Act other than the foregoing has not been complied with. MCA s. 3 provides (1) Subject to the provision of this section, a marriage that takes place after the commencement of this Act is void in any of the following cases but not otherwise, that to say, where (a) either of the parties is, at the time of the marriage lawfully married to some other person; (b) the parties are within the prohibited degrees of consanguinity or, subject to section 4 of this Act, or affinity; (c) the marriage is not valid marriage under the law of the place where the marriage takes place, by reason of a failure to comply with the requirements of the law of that place with respect to the form of solemnization of marriages; (d) the consent of either of the parties is not a real consent because—(i) it was obtained by duress or fraud; or (ii) that party is mistaken as to identity of the other party, or as to the nature of the ceremony performed; or (iii) that party is mentally incapable of understanding the nature of the marriage contract.; (e) either of the parties is not of marriageable age.

[157] For example blood relationship, social status, etc. This is normally revealed during the prelim enquires (supra) which always preceded the celebration of customary law marriage in Nigeria.

every marriage celebration. This is carried out by the parties and their respective families. The reason for this investigation is to find if there is any thing on the way to a valid celebration of customary marriage. It is also geared towards establishing the freedom of the parties to marry or not to marry.

2.1.5 INSTRUCTIONS FOR THE COUPLE ON MARRIAGE

The demand for a formal requirement for the celebration of marriage is also aimed at giving the couple concerned proper instruction on marriage. It offers the opportunity to counsel the parties about the key elements of the marriage they are about to celebrate.

Under the Canonical form, the parties are instructed on the nature of the canonical marriage and their obligations in the marriage. The sanctity of the marriage is explained. This is further buttressed by the use of sacred rites and places for the celebration of the marriage.

Under the Statutory form the Registrar of marriage offers instructions to the intended couples as they come to celebrate their marriage. The civil officer of marriage must under pain of penalty explain to the intended couples the obligations of the marriage they are about to celebrate.

Under the Customary law, the head of family give instructions to the intended couples with regard to their obligations in marriage and the duty to keep the tradition of their ancestors.

This instruction on marriage probably might not be given where there is no formal requirement for the celebration of marriage. The key witnesses to the marriage namely, the official witness in the case of the Church, the marriage registrar or the ministers of religion in the case of the State, and the head of the family in case of the customary law marriage are under obligation to offer this instruction on marriage to the intended parties.

2.2 THE BASIC SIMILARITIES AND DISSIMILARITIES IN THE CANONICAL, STATUTORY AND CUSTOMARY FORMS

The similarities and differences in the Canonical, Nigeria Statutory and Nigeria Customary form could be investigated along the following lines.

1. Preliminary investigations
2. Public celebration before witnesses
3. Places and times of celebrations
4. Some form of record of the celebration;
5. Dispensations from the formal requirement of marriage celebration;
6. Forms that affects validity and forms that deals only with lawfulness of the celebration.

2.2.1 PRELIMINARY INVESTIGATIONS

This is primary in the canonical, statutory and customary form. Under the canonical form, this is carried out by the use of banns published in the parishes of the parties to the marriage. Under the Statutory, this is done by the marriage registrar fixing the notice of the intended marriage at the marriage registrar's office for a period of twenty one days. Under the customary law, this is carried out by the parties and their families respectively.

The goal of this investigation is the same in the three laws namely, to establish the freedom of the parties to enter into a valid and lasting marriage. But the manner and ways of carrying out the investigation differs as stated above. Thus we have the case of common goal and different methods.

2.2.2 PUBLIC CELEBRATIONS BEFORE WITNESSES

The three systems are unanimous in the demand of a public celebration of marriage as an essential formal requirement. This celebration must be done before witnesses.

Under the canonical system of the Latin rite, the witness must include one official witness of the Church. This is normally the ordinary or the pastor. But they could delegate another priest or deacon to serve as an official witness of the Church. Under certain circumstances, the diocesan bishop could delegate a lay person to serve as an official witness of the Church.

In addition to the official witness there must be at least two other witnesses. These must be persons with adequate use of reason who are capable of testifying to the fact of marriage being celebrated in their presence.

The canonical form of the Latin Code also admits of the possibility of the use of an extraordinary form which allows for the celebration of marriage in the presence of at least two witnesses without an official witness.

The canonical form in the Eastern code also provides for public celebration in the presence of an official witness of the Church and at least two others. The official witness here is the priest (hierarch or pastor or other priests delegated by either of them). The deacon and lay-persons cannot serve as official witness under the Eastern code. This is because of the requirement of the sacred rites attached to the form. The blessing of the priest is an essential and integral part of the canonical form of Eastern Christians. This blessing can only be given by the priest and not by any other person. Thus deacons (and also laypersons) lack the faculty to bless marriages in Oriental Catholic and non-Catholic Churches.[158] The Eastern code allows for the use of extraordinary form. But where such is the case, the couples concerned must seek the blessing of the priest as soon as possible.

The Statutory form made provision for celebrations also before an officer recognized by the State and at least two witnesses.

The Customary form insists on the presence of certain persons to perform the rites for the celebration of marriage. If this is not the case, the marriage is invalid. The publicity of the customary form is demonstrated by the fact that it must be celebrated before the family members of the parties.[159]

In conclusion, marriage must be performed before a recognized officer and other witnesses. The goal is to make the certainty of the celebration of the marriage indubitable. However, the officer recognized as such under the three laws differs. Here again we have the case of same goal, different methods.

2.2.3 PLACES AND TIMES OF CELEBRATION

Marriages under the Latin Code are celebrated in the parish where either of the parties has domicile, quasi-domicile or month-long residence; if they are transients in the actual place where they reside; or elsewhere

---

[158] Prader, op.cit., pp. 136-137; Faris, J.D., *Canonical issues in the pastoral care of Eastern Catholics,* in CLSA, Proceedings of the fifty.third Annual convention, San Antonio, Texas, October 14-17, 1991, (Washington D.C:, 1992), p.164.

[159] By family members here is meant not the nuclear family as it operates in the western world but the extended family as it is envisioned in the African context.

with the permission of the proper Ordinary or pastor.[160] Under the Oriental Code, marriages are celebrated before the pastor of the groom, unless particular law determines otherwise or a just cause excuses.[161]

In both cases, marriage must be celebrated in the parish Church or other sacred places with the permission of the Ordinary or the parish priest.[162]The celebration of marriage under the Codes at the parish church shows the sacredness attached to marriage which is viewed as a sacrament. It also portrays a sense of community of the couple with other members of the parish family.

Canonical marriage could take place any time within the year and anytime during the day provided it is convenient to do so. However, canon 838 §2 CCEO states that particular laws of the various Churches *sui iuris* could give time for the celebration of marriage.

With the *Marriage Act* in Nigeria, Statutory marriage must be celebrated either at the Registrar's office, a licensed place of worship, or the place named in the Minister's license. Marriages celebrated in any other place are null and void.[163]

Statutory marriage could be celebrated at any time of the year. But it must be celebrated at specified times of the day for it to be valid. If the celebration is to take place at the marriage registrar's office, it must take place between the hours of ten o'clock in the forenoon and four o'clock in the afternoon with the doors open. If the celebration is taking place in a licensed place of worship it must occur between the hours of eight o'clock in the forenoon and six o'clock in the afternoon, with the doors open.

---

[160] *CIC 1983*, c. 1115,
[161] *CCEO*, c. 831 § 2.
[162] *CIC 1983*, c. 1118 §1; *CCEO*. c. 838.
[163] MA, s. 33.

If the statutory marriage is to be celebrated in a place named in the Minister's license, it must be done between eight o'clock in the forenoon and six o'clock in the afternoon. The celebration must strictly comply with formalities that normally follow marriages performed at the licensed place of worship or the registrar's office.[164]

Customary marriages are normally celebrated at the home of the bride or the head of the family of the bride. There are no fixed times either of the year or of the day for the celebration. The time for the celebration depends on the convenience of the parties and their family members.

2.2.4 RECORD OF THE CELEBRATION

The canonical, statutory and customary laws requires as part of the formal requirements for the celebration of marriage a form of registration of the marriage celebrated. This is necessary to keep a public record of the marriage that has taken place. The public record of marriage celebrated completes the goal of preventing secret marriages.

The pastor has to make sure this is done under the code. The registrar under the statutes maintains the register. The customary courts in Nigeria now have the mandate to make sure that customary marriages are put on record.

2.2.5 DISPENSATION FROM THE FORMAL REQUIREMENT OF CELEBRATION OF MARRIAGE

Under the canonical form, dispensation is possible. A baptized practicing catholic could be dispensed from observing the canonical form in the celebration of his or her marriage by the appropriate

---

[164] MA, s. 29.

authority. Under the statutory form the only dispensation possible is that of not obtaining the registrar's certificate. But in its place, the Minister's license must be obtained and all other formalities for the celebration of marriage are to be strictly adhered to. The customary law marriage does not allow of situations where a valid customary marriage could take place without the observance of the customary formalities.

2.2.6 FORMS THAT AFFECTS VALIDITY AND FORM THAT DEALS WITH LAWFULNESS ONLY

There are formal requirements for the celebration of marriage that deals with the validity of the marriage. Others deal with the lawfulness of the celebration of marriage.

A form required for validity renders the marriage invalid if celebrated without its observance. But a form required for lawfulness does not render the marriage invalid when it is not observed.

Under the canonical form, a marriage is invalid if celebrated in the absence of the proper official witness and at least two other persons. The same is true under the statutory system.

Canon law admits situations where a marriage could be validly celebrated in the absence of the official witness but in the presence of at least two other witnesses. This is called the extraordinary form. The Statutory system and the customary system in Nigeria do not observe such a form. Statutory marriage under all conditions must be conducted before the marriage registrar or an officer recognized by the government and at least two witnesses. The customary marriage must be performed by the head of the bride's family or his representative in the presence of other family members. When this is not the case, the marriage will be considered invalid.

Under the canonical system, the place of celebration of the marriage has no bearing on the validity of the marriage. It affects only the lawfulness of the celebration of marriage. Thus if a pastor assists in a marriage in the parish hall or any other place apart from the church or a sacred place in the presence of two witnesses, the marriage will be valid nonetheless. But under the statutory law system, the Registrar cannot validly officiate at a marriage in any other place apart from the Registrar's office or the place named in the Minister's license. Marriages performed outside the registrar's office or a license place of worship or in the place named in the minister's license is *ipso facto null and void ab initio.* The place of celebration of marriage is therefore of essence in determining the validity of marriage under the statutory law.

In the customary law system, it is surely the case that marriage celebrations that took place outside the house of the bride or a place chosen by the families of the bride might not be considered marriage in accordance with customary law. Thus it will be unheard of to say that a customary marriage took place where the bride's family did not approve. Such will be short of the requirement of a customary law marriage.

Under the Canonical system, lack of registration of the marriage that has taken place does not affect the validity of the marriage. The same is the case under the statutory law. But under some customary laws in Nigeria, non registration of customary law marriage renders it null and void.

2.3   PROBLEM CAUSED BY THE MULTIPLICITY OF FORMS OF MARRIAGE CELEBRATION IN NIGERIA

At this point, it is clear that there exist in Nigeria different forms for the celebration of different types of marriages. The canonical forms govern the canonical marriage. The statutory forms govern the statutory marriage. The customary forms govern the customary marriage.

A Catholic in Nigeria who intends to celebrate a valid marriage is faced with problems. He belongs to a tribe in Nigeria. He will like his marriage to be recognized by his tribal kinsmen and women. He is therefore obligated to perform the customary formalities enumerated above in the previous chapter for the celebration of his marriage. Being a Catholic he would want his marriage to be valid in the eyes of the Church. For the same marriage for which he has performed the customary formalities, he adds the canonical formalities in line with the provisions of the canon law. But since marriages of Catholics conducted solely according to canon law without fulfilling the requirements of the *Marriage Act* is not civilly recognized in Nigeria, he will be obliged also to observe the statutory mandatory formalities. At the end of the day, he will have to celebrate his marriage observing the requirements of the customary law, the canon law and the statutory law.

This practice is burdensome for the Catholic parties. It takes a lot of time to observe the requirements of the different forms. Certain formalities are repeated in different ways. The customary enquiry for example will still be followed by the registrar's investigations and then the pastor's enquiry. This takes a lot of time.

Apart from the time factor and repetitive nature of the forms involved, it also cost a lot of money. For the same marriage, the parties will have to run the customary expenses, then the statutory expenses and the Church expenses.

To make the whole matter worst, when all these things are done, the parties to the marriage get confused with regard to the proper law that should govern their marriage. They run from the customary law to the statutory law and to the church law to seek solutions to problems in their marriage with conflicting consequences.

Something has to be done to prevent this celebration of church marriage preceded by the customary and statutory formalities with its problems.

2.4. PROPOSAL TO OVERCOME THE PROBLEMS

Legal luminaries of International repute in Nigeria have suggested ways to overcome the problems created by the multiplicity of forms of marriage celebration in Nigeria.

Professor Agbede of the Faculty of Law, University of Lagos in an article titled "Towards evolving a single marriage law in Nigeria: Prospects and problems in the conflict of laws"[165] argued for a fusion of marriage laws in Nigeria by harmonization. The main trust of his argument is the creation of a system whereby polygamous and monogamous marriages could be contracted under one statute law on marriage.

Dr. Bamidele Oyebanji also of the Faculty of Law, University of Lagos in an article captioned "Proposals for reform of marriage laws in Nigeria"[166] perceived injustice in the lack of uniformity in marriage laws in Nigeria. For him, a situation whereby marriage under the marriage statutes is monogamous and that under the customary law is polygamous is a ground for injustice. He therefore advocated for a marriage law in Nigeria whereby monogamy will be the order of the day but with a caveat. His proposed legal reform of marriage which will be in line with "Article 31 of the Moroccan Code of Personal Status to the effect that marriage is a contract and a woman can stipulate in her marriage contract that her husband shall not take a

---

[165]   in Aguda, T.A. (ed.), *The Marriage Laws of Nigeria,* (Lagos: Nigeria Institute of Advanced Legal Studies, 1981), pp. 137-146l.

[166]   Ibid. pp. 147-166.

co-wife, and if the husband should fail to honor this pledge she is entitled to a divorce or to live apart."[167]

These legal suggestions propose a uniform system of marriage law in Nigeria. They argued from the point of view of the seemingly discrimination between parties who contracted marriage under the Act and persons who contracted marriage under the customary law. They did not address the fundamental issue of the nature of the marriages involved. For example they said nothing about the sacramental and religious nature of marriages contracted according to the norms of canon law by many Nigerians.

2.4.1 IMPOSSIBILITY OF HAVING ONE SINGLE FORM OF MARRIAGE CELEBRATION IN NIGERIA

Is it possible to have one single form of marriage celebration in Nigeria in order to avoid the multiplicity of forms of celebration? Our opinion is that this cannot be possible and it is not even advisable. The reasons for so stating include the following:

1. Difference in the nature of marriages involved.
2. Difference in the law-givers
3. Difference in the court systems
4. Difference in the formal requirements for the celebration of marriage.

2.4.1.1 DIFFERENCES IN THE NATURE OF MARRIAGES INVOLVED

Marriages under consideration in Nigeria here are the canonical marriage, the statutory marriage and the customary marriage. Now

---

[167] Ibid. p. 161.

these marriages are very distinct in their nature. They cannot be loped into one. Let us have a brief look at their basic natures.

Marriage under the Marriage Act in Nigeria and marriage in canon law are basically monogamous. They exist between one man and one woman to the exclusion of all others. They are ordered towards the good of the couple and for procreation and education of children.

Even though they have the common nature of monogamy, there are certain essential differences between them. First, statutory marriage is a civil marriage while marriage under canon law is a religious marriage.

Secondly, Marriage under canon law is a sacrament. This is so because marriage between the baptized[168] has been raised by Christ the Lord to the dignity of a "sacrament".[169] Accordingly, a valid marriage contract cannot exist between baptized persons without its being by that very fact a sacrament.[170]

Marriage of Roman Catholics is perceived as a vocation. Only those who are called to it can embrace it.[171]. It is a way to salvation for those who are in it. Through the fulfillment of the obligations attached to the marital life, couples will be rewarded both in this life and in the life to come.

---

[168] A baptized person is one who has received the sacrament of baptism in accordance with the Trinitarian formula laid down by Jesus Christ; See Matthew 28: 19-20.

[169] *CIC 1983* c.1055 §1.A sacrament by the Church definition is an outward sign of inward grace, ordained by Jesus Christ by which grace is given to our soul. *The Catechism of the Catholic Church,* Ibadan: Pauline Publications, 1994, no.1131.

[170] *CIC 1983*, c. 1055 §2.

[171] Matthew 19: 10-12.

Marriage under the Act is perceived as a contract of an extraordinary nature in the sense that it creates a status. Marriage under canon law is also seen in that light. But above all, it is better described as a covenant.[172] Covenant here is used in the religious sense. It is a bond of a sacred nature that binds two parties. In the Catholic tradition, the marriage covenant is likened to the covenant between God and Abraham, God and Israel in the Old Testament of the Hebrew Scriptures and the covenant between Jesus Christ and the Church in the New Testament. [173]

Further more, marriage under canon law has two indispensable characters namely, unity and indissolubility. [174] For marriage under the Act indissolubility is not a major character. Although the marriage union under the Act is meant to be for life, it does not imply that the marriage cannot be terminated by means other than by death of a party. It can be lawfully brought to an end by a decree of a competent civil court.[175]

---

[172] *CIC 1983*, c. 1055.

[173] Genesis: 12: 1.9, Genesis 15 & 17; Exodus 19-21; Ephesians 4: 22-23.

[174] By unity is meant that the couple should be joined to form one flesh no longer two. And by indissolubility is meant that the marriage bond should subsist for better for worse, for richer for poorer, in health and in sickness until death. A practical reason for the doctrine of indissolubility of marriage is that it is very difficult for one spouse to raise children properly. Again, a spouse needs care as his or her strength wanes. It takes 20 to 30 years to raise a family, a good part of the life s pan of a marriage. The law that requires their staying together until death is a great help for stability of the home and family. Besides there is something about the nature of sacred married love, which requires that, the bond between husband and wife is unbreakable until death. In 1 Corinthians 7:39, couples are enjoined to live together as far as they are alive. But if one dies, the surviving party has the right to remarry provided it is in the Lord.

[175] Nwogugu, *Family Law in Nigeria,* op. cit., p. xxxi.

Lastly, it must be stressed that marriage of Catholics, even if one party is baptized, is governed not only by divine law but also by canon law, without prejudice to the competence of the civil authority in respect of the merely civil effects of the marriage.[176]

Customary law marriage in Nigeria on the other hand is potentially polygamous by nature. It allows for the practice of one man having more than one wife. The opposite practice of one woman having more than one husband is an abomination under the customary law.[177] Customary law marriage permits divorce.

From the fore going it is clear that the nature of canonical marriage, statutory marriage and customary marriage are distinct and different from each other. It is wrong to say that because marriage under canon law is monogamous, that it is the same as marriage under the Act.

2.4.1.2   DIFFERENCE IN THE LAW-GIVERS

The authority responsible for the enactment of laws that governs the marriages differs.

The law that governs the universal Church is given by the supreme authority in the Church. The supreme authority in the Church is formed by the Roman Pontiff,[178] and the college of bishops in communion with him.[179] Only the supreme authority in the church could promulgate laws including marriage laws which bind all Catholics.

---

[176]   *CIC 1983*, c. 1059.

[177]   See the case of *Kpelanya v. Tsoka and Anor,* NNLR, (1971), 86, where the court ruled that under Tiv customary law a woman could not lawfully be married to two men at the same time.

[178]   *CIC 1983*, c. 331

[179]   Ibid. c. 336.

In Nigeria, the authority vested with the regulations of the statutory marriage is the Federal legislature. The constitution of the Federal Republic of Nigeria vested exclusive legislative competence on the National Assembly on issues regarding "the formation, annulment and dissolution of marriages other than marriages under Islamic law and customary law including matrimonial causes relating thereto."[180]

The authority that provides the norms that governs the customary law marriages is found in the various tribal customs in Nigeria. Each tribe has group of traditional rulers and elders that try to help their people keep to the custom of their ancestors. Customary law of marriage is thus native and customary to the people. The government clearly removes its hand from issues dealing with customary law marriage.[181]

2.4.1.3   DIFFERENCES IN THE COURT SYSTEMS

The marriages whose forms we are comparing have different Courts that deal with matters relating to them. In Nigeria, the customary law marriages fall within the exclusive jurisdiction of the customary courts. The Statutory marriages under the high courts, while the canon law marriages are taken care of by the marriage tribunals of the Catholic Church.

2.4.1.3.1   COURTS FOR CUSTOMARY LAW MARRIAGES IN NIGERIA

Matters relating to marriages contracted under the customary law are first and foremost handled by the customary courts which exist in all the states of Nigeria. Customary courts are established primarily for the administration of customary law.

---

[180]   *Constitution of the Federal Republic of Nigeria*, 1999, Exclusive Legislative list, item, 61

[181]   Ibid.

In the states that falls within the former Northern region of Nigeria, they are referred to as area courts. In Cross River state, they are called district courts.[182] While in the states of the western region and the eastern region they are referred to as customary courts.

The customary courts in each State of the federation of Nigeria have unlimited jurisdiction in civil cases arising under customary law. These include matrimonial cases and cases relating to children under customary law.

Customary courts are governed by the customary court laws of the various states in Nigeria. In Lagos state for example, the customary court law provides for the establishment of customary courts by the Attorney-general of the State by a warrant.[183] The court is composed of "a President and at least two or other four members as the case may be."[184]

The Customary court in Lagos State have unlimited civil jurisdiction in "matrimonial causes and other matters between persons married under customary law or arising from or connected with a union contracted under customary law, that is matrimonial causes and related matters under customary law."[185]

In the other states of the former western region of Nigeria, the applicable law that governs the customary courts is the Customary Court Law.[186] The customary courts in these states have civil

---

[182] It should be noted that the notion of district court in Cross Rivers state which is akin to customary court is different from the notion of district courts in the Northern states of Nigeria which is equivalent to magistrates' courts in the Southern part of Nigeria.

[183] *Lagos Laws* 1973, cap.33, s. 1 (1).

[184] Ibid. s. 2.

[185] Ibid. s. 15 and Schedule 2, pt 1

[186] *Western Region of Nigeria Laws*, 1959, cap. 31.

jurisdiction in "matrimonial causes and matters between persons married under customary law or arising from or connected with a union contracted under customary law."[187] It excludes "any cause or matter relating to; arising from or connected with a Christian marriage as defined in section 1 of the Criminal Code"[188]

In the States that falls to the former Northern region of Nigeria, customary courts are designated as area courts. The applicable laws that govern the area courts are the various *Area Courts Edicts* in force in the respective states. These are basically uniform in their legislations.

An area court in a state is established by warrant by the Chief Judge of the state.[189] There are four classes of area courts, namely, *Upper Area Courts, Area Courts Grade I, Area Courts Grade II, and Area Courts Grade III*.[190] All the grades of the Area Courts have unlimited original jurisdiction in "matrimonial causes and matters between persons married under customary law or arising from or connected with a union contracted by customary law other than those arising from or connected with a Christian marriage as defined in S. 1 of the Criminal Code."[191]

---

[187] *Western Region of Nigeria Laws*, 1959, cap. 31, s. 18 and Schedule 2, (Pts. 1-111) as amended by s. 16 of the Customary Courts (Amendment) Edict 1972 (Western States).

[188] Criminal Code, *Western Region Nigeria Laws* 1959, cap.28, define "Christian marriage" as "a marriage which is recognized by the law of the place where it is contracted as the voluntary union for life of one man and one woman to the exclusion of all others. A marriage under the Marriage Act is a Christian marriage within the meaning of the Code."

[189] See e.g. Benue-Plateau State—*Area Courts Edict,* 1968, s. 3 (1).

[190] Ibid. S. 17.

[191] Benue-Plateau State—*Area Court Edict,* 1968, s. 3 (2).

In Cross Rivers State which was carved out of the East Central State[192] customary court was designated as district courts. It was established by the warrant of the Military governor of the State. It exercises original unlimited civil jurisdiction among other matters in cases relating to "matrimonial causes and matters between persons married under customary law or arising from or connected with a union contracted under customary law, the jurisdiction being unlimited; and cases relating to the custody of children under customary law, the jurisdiction being unlimited."[193]

In the East Central States of Nigeria, customary courts were formally abolished in 1971 and their jurisdiction taken over by the Magistrates' Courts and the High Courts.[194] But with the Federal government directives of 1978[195] the Customary Courts were re-introduced in the affected states namely Anambra, Bendel, Imo and Rivers states. The have original unlimited jurisdiction in civil matters including matrimonial causes and cases relating to children under the customary law.

From the fore going, it is clear that customary courts operates in all the States of the federation of Nigeria with original unlimited civil jurisdictions in marriages contracted under the customary law.

Appeal from the Customary Courts goes to the Customary Court of Appeal. Those from the Area Courts go to the Upper Area Courts. Further appeals from the Upper Area Courts go to the Sharia Court of Appeal in those matters that involves purely Moslem personal law where parties to the proceedings are Muslims.[196]

---

[192] See *the States (Creation and Transitional Provisions) Decree,* 1976.

[193] *Local Courts Interim Judicial Service Bodies (Establishment, etc) Decree* 1978, s. 12 (1).

[194] *High Court (Amendment) Edict,* 1971, s. 3.

[195] See "White Paper on the Federal Military Government's Views on the Report of the Customary Courts Reform Committee," Lagos, 1978.

[196] *Laws of Northern Nigeria,* 1963, cap. 122, s.224.

The Constitution of the Federal Republic of Nigeria 1979 made provision for the establishment of Customary Court of Appeal in each State of the Federation.[197] The Customary Court of Appeal has appellate jurisdiction in civil cases involving questions of customary law.

The 1989 Constitution made the establishment of the Customary Court of Appeal optional in the states of the federation.[198]

The 1999 Constitution which is the supreme law in force in Nigeria today provides for the Customary Court of Appeal thus "there shall be for any state that requires it a Customary Court of Appeal for that State".[199] The jurisdiction of the Customary Court of appeal includes the exercise of "appellate and supervisory jurisdiction in civil proceedings involving questions of customary law".[200]

The 1999 constitution also made the establishment of Sharia Court of Appeal optional for the States.[201] The Sharia Court of Appeal has appellate and supervisory jurisdiction in civil proceedings involving questions of Islamic Law where all the parties are Muslims.[202]

Further appeals from the Customary Court of Appeal or the Sharia Court of Appeal lies to the Federal Court of Appeal referred to simply as the Court of Appeal.[203] The Court of Appeal is made up of a president and a number of Justices, not less than fifteen, at least three

---

197 *Constitution of the Federal Republic of Nigeria*, 1979, s. 245 (1)
198 *Constitution of the Federal Republic of Nigeria*, 1989, s. 264 states "there shall be for any State that requires it a Customary Court of Appeal for the State".
199 *Constitution of the Federal Republic of Nigeria*, 1999, s. 280 (1).
200 Ibid.
201 *Constitution of the Federal Republic of Nigeria*, 1999, s. 275 (1).
202 Ibid. s. 277.
203 *Constitution of the Federal Republic of Nigeria*, 1999, s. 240.

of whom must be learned in Islamic Law, and at least a further three leaned in Customary Law.[204]

A further appeal from the Court of Appeal goes to the Supreme Court of Nigeria. [205] The decision of the Supreme Court is final.[206]

It should be noted here that the Law administered by the Customary Courts are the native laws and customs prevailing in the area of the jurisdiction of the court provided they are not repugnant to natural justice, equity and good conscience[207] and does not contradict any written law in force at the time.

It should further be observed that in matters involving purely customary laws in the North of Nigeria where the Area Courts are in operation, appeals lies to the Upper Area Courts. Appeals from the Upper Area Courts do not go to the Sharia Court of Appeal unless it involves question of Islamic personal law and the parties are Muslims. Where should appeal from purely customary law marriages from the Upper Area Courts in the North lie in cases which does not involves Islamic personal law and the parties are not Muslims? Appeals from the Upper Area Court in such cases will no doubt go to the High Court of the State or directly to the Court of Appeal. The Law in Nigeria is yet to address the issue.

---

[204] Ibid. s.237 (2) (b) The fact that at least three of the justices of the court must be learned in Customary law and three in Islamic law is necessary by virtue of the appeal coming from the customary court of appeal and the Sharia Court of Appeal.

[205] *Constitution of the Federal Republic of Nigeria,* 1999, s. 233 (1).

[206] Ibid. s. 235 states "Without prejudice to the powers of the President or of the Governor of a State with respect to prerogative of mercy, no appeal shall lie to any other body or person from any determination of the Supreme Court."

[207] See *Supreme Court Ordinance,* 1876, s. 19, which empower courts to apply "native law or custom" not "repugnant to natural justice, equity and good conscience."

It should be noted also that there are certain exceptional circumstances whereby matters dealing with the customary law are handled at the first instance by the Magistrates' Courts or the High Courts. Professor *Nwogugu*[208] pointed out three situations where such could be the case. One scenario is when a Military governor under a Military regime, which is not infrequent in Nigeria, directs by an order that a matter or matters of customary law be treated by the Magistrates Courts or the High Courts. The second scenario is where a suit is transferred to the High Court or the Magistrates' Court; they can exercise original jurisdiction in the suit. The third situation is an unusual case of the abolition of Customary Court, and then its jurisdiction will be transferred to the Magistrate Court or the High Court.[209] It should be noted that where customary and area courts exist, the High Courts have no original jurisdiction in specified customary law cases.[210]

Finally, it should be noted that even though Customary Courts in Nigeria deals with customary law marriages, in certain situation enumerated above matters of customary law marriages are handled by the Magistrates' Courts and the High courts. Ultimately, the Court of Appeal and the Supreme Court handle final appeals arising from suits involving customary law marriages. There is thus a merger of the customary courts with the civil (state) courts in Nigeria at the highest levels.

2.4.1.3.2 **COURTS FOR STATUTORY LAW MARRIAGES IN NIGERIA.**

The Federal Government of Nigeria has exclusive jurisdiction over matters relating to the 'formation, annulment and dissolution of

---

[208] Nwogugu, *Family Law in Nigeria,* op. cit., p. 118.

[209] *High Court (Amendment) Law,* (East Central States, 1974), s. 2; *Magistrates' Court (Amendment) Law,* (East Central State, 1971), s. 5.

[210] *High Court Law,* (Western Region, 1959), s. 9.

Marriages other than Marriages under Islamic law and customary law including the matrimonial causes relating thereto'.[211] In matters that deal with the statutory marriage in Nigeria, only the Federal Government could legislate.

The jurisdiction on Matrimonial Causes arising from Statutory Marriage has been conferred by the Federal Government on the State High Courts.[212] Magistrates' Courts or District Courts cannot entertain suits involving the Statutory Marriage. This latter courts could only be involved where the High Court in a proceeding ordered that certain thing be done; for example maintenance. They could then enforce payment in a summary manner when maintenance is ordered in proceedings in a High Court.[213] Other than the enforcement of an order of payment in maintenance proceedings, the Magistrates' Courts or the District Courts have no hand in matters dealing with Statutory Marriages.

The constitution of Nigeria provides for the establishment of State high courts in all the states of the Federation.[214] The High Courts among other matters exercises original jurisdiction in matters arising from Statutory Marriage.[215]

The jurisdiction of the High courts to deal with marriage contracted under the Act is based on domicile[216] or the place of residence of the

---

[211] *Constitution of the Federal Republic of Nigeria*, 1979, s. 4 and item 58 of the second Schedule (Pt. 1) of the Exclusive Legislative List.

[212] *Regional Courts (Federal Jurisdiction) Act*, s. 3; this Act is now known as *State Courts (Federal Jurisdiction), Act*. See also s. *MCA*, 1970, s.2 (1) which confer jurisdiction in matrimonial causes on the high court of every state of the Federation.

[213] *MCA*, 1970, ss. 2 (1) and 114 (1)

[214] *Constitution of the Federal Republic of Nigeria*, 1999, s. 270.

[215] *MCA*, s.2 (1).

[216] *MCA* s. 2 (2).

parties. For the purpose of marriage under the Marriage Act the entire federation of Nigeria constitutes one single domicile.[217] This means that any one who contract marriage under the *Marriage Act* could institute proceedings in any high court of any state of the federation whether he or she is actually living in the state or not.[218]

Appeals from the state High Courts as of right go straight to the Court of Appeal. Further appeals from the Court of Appeal go to the Supreme Court.

2.4.1.3.3 COURTS FOR CANON LAW MARRIAGES

The Church has authority over marriages of all the baptized Catholics.[219] Marriages contracted with the canonical form are governed by the divine law and the provision of the Code of canon law with reference to the civil authorities in matters dealing with the civil effects of marriage.[220]

The code of canon law provides that the marriage cases of the baptized are to be handled by an ecclesiastical judge.[221] The ecclesiastical judge in the first instance is the diocesan bishop.[222] The diocesan bishop can exercise his judicial power through the judicial vicar[223] who constitutes

---

[217] *MCA* s.2 (3).
[218] In *Adegoroye v Adegoroye*, (1996), 2 NWLR, 712 the fact that the entire country of Nigeria constitutes one jurisdiction un the Matrimonial Causes Act was affirmed by the court. It should be noted also that the *Australia's Matrimonial Causes Act*, 1959, s. 23 had a similar view. The Nigerian Act borrowed from it.
[219] *CIC, 1983* c. 1059
[220] Ibid.
[221] *CIC 1983*, c. 1671.
[222] Ibid., c. 1419.
[223] *CIC 1983*, c. 1420 §1.

one tribunal with him.[224] The bishop also appoints diocesan judges[225] to serve at the diocesan tribunal. The diocesan tribunals in the first instance handle matters dealing with the determination of canonical marriages. The code however transfers to the civil courts all matters that connect the merely civil effects of the marriage unless particular law determines otherwise.[226] In such cases the code of canon law canonizes civil legislations.

Appeals lie from the diocesan tribunal of the first instance to the tribunal of the second instance. This is normally a different tribunal from the first instance tribunal. The determination of the second instance tribunal is given by the code. From the tribunals of a suffragan bishop appeal goes to the metropolitan tribunal.[227] But if the metropolitan is the first instance tribunal, appeals goes to the tribunal that is permanently designated with the approval of the Holy See.[228] In cases where a single first instance tribunal is established by different dioceses, appeals go to the tribunal of second instance established by the conference of bishops with the approval of the Holy See.[229]

Further appeals from the marriage cases handled by the second instance tribunals go directly to the Roman Rota.[230] The Roman Rota is the highest court of appeal under the code with respect to marriage contracted under the code of canon law.

Appeals do not lie from the marriage tribunals to the Court of Appeal in Nigeria or the Supreme Court of Nigeria but to the Roman Rota. This is an indication that in matters that deal with the substance of

---

[224] Ibid. §2.
[225] *CIC 1983*, c. 1421.
[226] Ibid., c. 1672.
[227] *CIC 1983*, c. 1438 1°.
[228] Ibid., c. 1438 2°.
[229] *CIC 1983*, c. 1439 § 1.
[230] Ibid., c. 1405 §3, 3°.

the canonical marriage, the civil courts in Nigeria have no hand. Thus the marriage tribunals of the dioceses of Nigeria and consequently the Roman Rota are not subject to the State Courts. State Courts only come into play where the code of cannon law referred issues to them. Otherwise, they are inoperative.

2.4.1.4 DIFFERENCES IN THE FORMAL REQUIREMENTS FOR THE CELEBRATION OF MARRIAGE.

The differences in the forms for the celebration of marriages under the canonical, statutory and customary law have been sufficiently exposed in all the previous chapters.[231] The canonical forms for the celebration of marriage involves celebration before a pastor or ordinary or the priest or deacon delegated by either of them, and in some cases the layperson delegated by the local ordinary in the presence of two witnesses.

The statutory form involves celebration before the registrar of marriage or an officer recognized under the Marriage Act and two witnesses.

The Customary form involves celebrations which include giving and receiving of the "marriage token" and the formal handing over of the bride to the groom.

In all the three forms of marriage celebrations, the officers are different. The places of celebrations are different. The activities on the occasion of the celebration also differ. Each is very unique.

---

[231] See Chapters two and three in particular for the specific forms of marriage under the canon, Nigeria statutory and customary laws.

2.4.2 THE WAY OUT: CIVIL RECOGNITION OF CANONICAL MARRIAGE

It is not possible and it is not even advisable to have a single form for the celebration of marriage under the canon, Nigeria statutory and customary laws. The reasons are as we have stated above.[232] We therefore recommend civil recognition of canonical marriage as the best way to come out of the problem created by the multiplicity of forms of marriage celebration in Nigeria.

The Church has always recognized statutory or customary marriages among non-Catholics as valid marriages. Catholics are bound to observe the canonical forms for their marriage to be valid in the eyes of the Church. It remains the State and the customary authorities to recognize marriages of which at least a party is a Catholic celebrated purely according to the canonical form without reference to the State and customary norms as valid.

Although the *Marriage Act* made reference to the minister of religion and licensed place of worship in the celebration of marriage, such marriage performed by the minister of religion are never regarded in the eyes of the law of Nigeria as canonical or religious marriage. They are seen as statutory marriage. In fact there is no such a thing as canonical marriage in the legal vocabulary of Nigeria. This is why the minister of religion is obliged to observe the precepts of the *Marriage Act* in the celebration of marriage or risk imprisonment. By so doing the State law limits the freedom of the Church when it comes to who should exchange valid marriage consent before its officials and the place such consents should be exchanged.

---

[232] The difference in the conception of marriage whereby one is potentially polygamous, the others monogamous but differs in sacrament and indissolubility. They have different law givers and different courts to address issues of the marriage. And ultimately, they have different requirements for formal celebration.

But with the civil recognition of the canonical marriage, Catholic parties who are bound to celebrate their marriage in accordance with the teachings of the Catholic Church, could simply approach their proper pastor or local ordinary and commence the process for the celebration of their marriage according to canon law with or without reference to the Statutory or customary laws. Their marriage will be celebrated in any place recognized by the canon law as a place for the celebration of marriage.

After the celebration, proper record of the marriage should be kept by the pastor and notification of same given to the registrar of marriage in the locality where the marriage was celebrated within a given period of time. The registrar of marriage will then note the fact of the celebration in his own record. The marriage celebrated should then be given full legal effect in Nigeria.[233]

The notification of the registrar of marriage of the marriage that has already been celebrated according to canon law does not limit the freedom of the Church with regard to persons who could exchange marriage consent before it. But the practice of obtaining the license of the registrar before the Church could officiate at marriage limits the freedom of the Church to marry only those who have gotten clearance from the State. This makes the Church an agent of the State and not an independent society caring for the needs of her faithful in accordance with her laws.

---

[233] This proposal is in line with the current practice in the Republic of Italy where there is a concordance between the Church and the State of Italy—see art. 34 of the *Concordat between the Holy See and Italy,* February,11, 1929. Similar practices are also found in Austria, Portugal, Spain and the Dominican Republic that signs accord with the Holy See. We do not need a concordance to make this work in Nigeria since the Muslim religion and customary law system in Nigeria have their marriages fully recognized by the law and there is no problem.

This proposal falls in place with the suggestion given at the end of the National workshop at the Nigerian Institute of Advanced Legal Studies Lagos, 1981 to wit having four separate and independent system of marriage in Nigeria namely, customary marriage, Islamic marriage, Christian marriage[234] and statutory marriage. Each marriage complying with laid down rules for each particular system. Each marriage being registered and a certificate issued only as evidence of the marriage. [235]

Acceptance of our proposal will accord legal status to canonical marriages celebrated in Nigeria without reference to the statutory and customary laws. Hitherto, marriages conducted purely according to canon law are regarded as of no legal consequence and as such null and void.[236]

2.4.3   REASONS IN SUPPORT OF THE PROPOSAL

We maintain this view because of the following reasons:

1. The pluralistic nature of the Nigerian society
2. The freedom of religion guaranteed by the Constitution of Nigeria
3. The current practice whereby Islamic marriages and customary law marriages are made independent of the Act.
4. The obvious advantages of the proposal.

---

[234] Christian marriage here means marriage between Christians. It should be noted that there are Christians of various denominations in Nigeria. The Catholic Church is the most prominent and operates canon law. The canonical marriage, that which involves at least a Catholic should stand for Catholics as the Christian marriage.

[235] Aguda, T.A., (ed.), *The Marriage Laws of Nigeria,* Lagos: The Nigerian Institute of Advanced Legal Studies, 1981, p. 168, appendix no. 4.

[236] *Obiekwe v Obiekwe,* ENLR, 7(1963),196; *Anyaegbunam v Anyaegbunam,* SC, 4 (1973), 121.The judicial law coming from these courts decisions have not changed. It is still the law in Nigeria.

2.4.3.1 PLURALISTIC NATURE OF THE NIGERIA SOCIETY

Nigeria is made up of diverse ethnic groups and tribes that speaks different languages and have different cultures. As indicated earlier, Nigeria has over two hundred and fifty ethnic nationalities that constituted it. These ethnic nationalities keep to their cultures and language.

The formation of Nigeria as one political entity in 1914[237] by the amalgamation of the Southern and Northern protectorate does not bring an end to this ethnic diversity, cultural and language differences. In fact the first constitution of Nigeria in 1954 acknowledges the fact of the multi-ethnicity of Nigeria.[238]

On account of these cultural and tribal differences in Nigeria, federalism is upheld as the system of government that can best serve the country. The reason for the adoption of federalism as the system of government in Nigeria as given by professor *Nwabueze* is to help each group govern itself in matters of local concern without interference or control by the others. It allows matters of common interest to be managed centrally; while those of both local and national concerns are handled concurrently. By so doing, the interest of each and every one of the group is guaranteed while at the same time balancing the peace and stability against the forces of division that is inherent in heterogeneous society.[239]

The best way therefore to make things work in Nigeria is to encourage its plural character. Stressing on this matter, the then head of state,

---

[237] *Nigeria Protectorate Order in Council*, 1913, art.4.

[238] *Nigeria (Constitution) Order in Council*, 1954, s.3.

[239] Nwabueze, B.O., *Federalism in Nigeria under the Presidential Constitution*, 1983, p.377

General *Ibrahim Babangida* in a nation wide broadcast of 3rd May 1989, said:

"The Armed Forces Ruling Council (A.F.R.C) took the view that only by firmly encouraging Nigeria's plural character within a federal system can our nation's stability be guaranteed for posterity . . . . We settled for federalism because we firmly believe that it is only through this that our diversity can be accommodated."[240]

Nigeria ethnic and cultural diversity was compounded by religious multiplicity. With exposure to the outside world, different religions of the world came to find their place in Nigeria. Thus we have Muslims, Christians of different denominations etc in Nigeria. These religious groups also came with their religious practices which binds their adherents in conscience.

To accommodate these religious practices and the diverse cultural practices in Nigeria it is pertinent that a system, which could accommodate all, be introduced. The federal system of government adopted in Nigeria accommodates these ethnic groups and the religious practices.

In line with the federal character of Nigeria, the customary law is allowed to govern the customary practices of the various ethnic groups in the society. The Muslim law is allowed to govern the Muslim in matters of personal Muslim concerns. The Catholic Church laws should therefore in our opinion be allowed to govern Catholics in matters of personal Catholic concerns. Hence the need for the civil recognition of Catholic marriages as separate entity independent of the Marriage Acts in Nigeria.

---

[240] *Lagos News* (Nigeria Newspaper), 4th May, 1989.

2.4.3.2 FREEDOM OF RELIGION GUARANTEED BY THE CONSTITUTION OF NIGERIA

The 1999 Constitution of the federal republic of Nigeria (and the previous federal constitutions) prohibits State Religion. It states that "the government of the Federation or of a State shall not adopt any religion as State religion".[241] The constitution further provides that "every person shall be entitled to freedom of thought, conscience and religion, including freedom to change his religion or belief, and freedom (either alone or in community with others, and in public or in private) to manifest and propagate his religion or belief in worship, teaching, practice and observance."[242]

Reading together these constitutional provisions, it is clear that the Catholic Church which is one of the dominant religious groups in Nigeria should be free to observe and practice her religion and faith. A key element in the practice of the religion of the Catholic Church is the observance of the marital laws of the Church. The Catholics are under obligation to follow their conscience and keep to the teachings of the Church with regard to marriage. Their understanding of marriage should not be distorted by the practices of people around them. Their conception of marriage should not be muddled with the secular concept of marriage under the statutory and customary laws. The freedom of religion granted by the constitution should avail them of the chance to celebrate their marriage without recourse to the state or the custom of the people but in line with the custom of the Church and divine law.

---

[241] *Constitution of the Federal Republic of Nigeria,*1999, s. 10.
[242] Ibid. s.38 (1).

2.4.3.3 CURRENT PRACTICE WHEREBY ISLAMIC MARRIAGES AND CUSTOMARY LAW MARRIAGES ARE MADE INDEPENDENT OF THE ACT

A further reason why we make the proposal is the fact that the Muslims in Nigeria who operates the Sharia law long ago have their religious marriages removed from the clutches of the state and local customs. Muslim marriages are governed purely by Muslim laws. They are celebrated in Nigeria without any reference to the provisions of the *Marriage Act.*

The Muslims claim that their religion is a way of life for the Muslims and their marriage should and must be governed by the Muslim or Sharia law. This is a sound reason. But every religion is also a way of life. The Catholic religion and faith is a way of life. Catholics are bound in conscience to observe the prescriptions of their religion in all matters of their personal daily life. It stands therefore to reason that marriages among Catholics or marriages of which a party is a Catholic and celebrated in accordance with the Church law be recognized in Nigeria as true and valid marriage with all legal consequences of marriage, just as the Muslim marriage and the customary law marriage. These are always celebrated without any recourse to the Nigeria statute on marriage.

2.4.3.4 ADVANTAGES OF THIS PROPOSAL

There are lots of obvious advantages that will flow from the civil recognition of the canonical marriage in Nigeria.

In the first place, the current practice whereby marriages contracted purely in accordance with the canonical forms are regarded as null and void in Nigeria will be averted.

It will prevent possible conflicts between the Church and the State. The situation whereby marriages celebrated purely according to the canonical form are declared null and void by the courts in Nigeria could result to the Catholics disregarding the court orders. Worst still, the local ordinary or pastor or their delegates who officiates in such marriage risk the danger of being incarcerated for violation of the State law. This is a potential conflict situation between the Church and the State. The yawning conflict will be prevented with the civil recognition of the canonical marriage.

Further, it will guarantee the freedom of Nigeria Catholics in the practice of their religion like the Nigerian Muslims. The canon law will then properly govern the formation of marriages of which at least a party is a Catholic.

Further still, it will save time and cost. The current practice of having a canonical marriage first preceded by the customary and statutory marriage will be averted. This practice of taking share in all the three forms of marriages kills time and is a lot of expense to the parties.

Lastly, the law to be followed will be clear. Parties will not be confused with respect to the proper law that governs their marriage. Clarity of the law will be achieved. The Catholics who have observed the customary form, the statutory form and the canonical form are often confused with respect to the proper law that governs their marriage. They usually run from customary to statutory then to canon law with conflicting consequences.[243]

---

[243] A typical example is a catholic couple who have marital problems. The civil court may grant them divorce. The customary law may not recognize the divorce unless the "marriage token" is return. The church tribunal may not find ground to declare the marriage invalid. The couple who have received divorce in the civil court will thus be left hanging. But if they were to contract their marriage purely in accordance with the canonical form which is civilly recognized as we

GENERAL CONCLUSION

Having run down the entire laws laid down for the formal celebration of the canonical marriage, statutory and customary marriage in Nigeria, one could make the following conclusions.

- Marriage exists between male and female persons. It assumes diverse forms among different social groups and religious confessions.
- The Marriage forms recognized in Nigeria are those celebrated in accordance with the Native laws and customs (customary law marriage); Islamic laws (Islamic law marriage); and Nigeria statutory laws (statutory law marriage or court marriage). The marriage celebrated in Roman Catholic Churches or in accordance with canon law, as a matter of obligation must follow the norms given in the Nigeria marriage statutes.
- There is in Nigeria no such a thing as canon law marriage (Christian marriage) which could be celebrated independent of the provisions of the *Marriage Act*.
- The laws that govern Statutory Marriage in Nigeria are contained in the *Marriage Act* and *the Matrimonial Causes Act.*
- Statutory law marriage in Nigeria could only be celebrated between a man and a woman to the exclusion of all others. The parties to the marriage are under obligation to obtain the registrar's certificate or the minister's license before the celebration of their marriage.
- Statutory law marriages are only celebrated before the registrar of marriage or the recognize minister of religion and two or

---

are proposing, they will know right from time that canon law and the divine law governs their marriage. They will not have any reason to approach the civil court or to return the "marriage token" as this might not be required. And should they approach the civil courts, the civil judge would direct them first to seek recourse in the Catholic tribunal which will then be the first and proper court to attend to their case.

more witnesses. It must be celebrated either at the Registrar's office or a licensed place of worship or the place named in the Minister's license following the norms laid down in the marriage statutes.

- Non-compliance with the provisions of the Act in the celebration of statutory law marriage renders it null and void.

- The statutory marriage and the customary law marriage are the only form of civil marriage known to the Nigeria law. It is therefore of utmost importance that parties to the marriage as well as ministers of religion be well informed of the formalities laid down for their valid celebrations.

- The customary law marriages are governed by the various customary laws that exist in Nigeria. They are potentially polygamous.

- The canon law marriage is governed by the divine law and canon law. This has no independent existence in Nigeria. It is falsely classified as statutory marriage.

- The classification of canon law marriage under statutory marriage has created a lot of problem.

- Even though they share the common element of 'monogamy', canon law conception of marriage is quite different from the statutory law conception of marriage.

- Marriage under canon law has laid out formalities for its celebration which binds all Catholics in conscience.

- The statutory marriage and the customary marriage in Nigeria also have distinct formalities for their celebration

- To avoid confusion of law and the problem that normally occurs when two different things are locked up together in one compartment; we advocate for the civil recognition of canonical marriage.

- This proposition is sound based on the fact that Nigeria as a multi ethnic and multi religious nation will function better if personal matters and issues dealing with religion and conscience are kept where they belong.

APPENDIXES

APPENDIX 1

NOTICE OF MARRIAGE—MA. S. 7
(FORM A, First schedule to the Marriage Act)

To the registrar of marriages for the _____ district of Nigeria

I hereby give you notice that a marriage is intended to be had within three months from the date hereof between me, the undersigned, and the other party herein named.

Name	Condition	Occupation, rank or profession	Age	Dwelling or place of abode	Consent, if any, and by whom given
Bridegroom	Bachelor or widower	Farmer, etc, (as case may be)	23		
Bride	Spinster or widow	Laundress (as case may be)	18		Father or Guardian

Witness my hand this _____ day of _____, 20_____

_____
Signature

APPENDIX 2

FORM OF ATTESTATION—MA. SS. 8 & 19
(FORM B, First schedule to the marriage Act)

Signed by the said _____ of _____ on the _____ day of _____ 20 _____, this notice having been first read over to him (her) (or read over and truly interpreted to him (her) in the _____ language) by _____. He (she) seemed to understand the same and made his (her) mark thereto in my presence.

_____

Signed

APPENDIX 3

REGISTRAR'S CERTIFICATE—MA. S. 11
(FORM C, First schedule to the Marriage Act)

I, _____, registrar of marriages in the _____ district of Nigeria, do hereby certify that on the _____ day of _____ notice was duly entered in the marriage notice book of this district, of the marriage intended between the parties herein named and described, such notice being delivered under the hand of the parties, that is to say.

Name	Condition	Occupation, rank or profession	Age	Consent	Dwelling	Length of residence
A.B.	Bachelor	Boatman (as the case may be)	19 (as the case may be)	E.F. the Father (as the case may be)		
C.D.	Spinster	(as case may be)	16 (as case may be)	G.H. the mother (as the case may be)		

Date of notice entered _____ 20 _____
Date of certificate given _____ 20 _____
No caveat has been entered against the issue of this certificate; or a caveat was entered against the issue of this certificate on the _____ day of _____ 20 _____, but it has been cancelled _____
Witness my hand this _____ day of _____ 20 _____

_____

A.B., Registrar of Marriages _____ District.
Note: This certificate will be void unless the marriage is solemnized on or before the _____ day of _____ 20 _____

_____

(A.B)

APPENDIX 4

SPECIAL LICENSE—MA S. 13
(FORM D, First schedule to the Marriage Act)

Whereas A.B. and C.D. desire to intermarry, and sufficient cause has been shown to me why the preliminaries required by the Marriage Ordinance should be dispensed with:

Now, therefore, in pursuance of the said Ordinance, I do dispense with the giving of notice and the issue of the certificate thereby prescribed, and do hereby authorize any registrar of marriages, or recognized minister of some religious denomination or body, to celebrate marriage between the said A.B. and C.D. at (place of celebration), between the hours of 8 o'clock in the forenoon and 6 o'clock in the afternoon, and within—days from the date hereof.

Given under my hand, this _____ day of _____ 20 _____

(Signed) _____

Governor

APPENDIX 5

MARRIAGE CERTIFICATE—MA. SS. 24 & 25
(FORM E, First schedule to the Marriage Act)

Marriage celebrated in the _____ at _____ in Nigeria
No. _____
Certificate of Marriage

—20—	No.	When married	Names and surnames	Full age or minor	Con dition	Rank or profession	Residence at time of marriage	Father's name and surname	Occupation or profession of Father
Name of Husband									
Name of Wife Witnesses									

Married at _____ by (or before) me _____,
(Minister or registrar as the case may be)
The marriage was celebrated between us _____ _____ in the
presence of.

_____   _____

Witnesses

APPENDIX 6

MARRIAGE REGISTER BOOK—MA. S. 30
(FORM F, First schedule to the Marriage Act)

When married	Names and surnames	Whether full age or minor	Condition	Occupation	Residence	Father's name and occupation

Entered this _____ day of _____ 20 _____ at the district registry of marriage at _____

(Signed)   A.B

_____

Registrar

APPENDIX 7

NOTICE OF FOREIGN MARRIAGE—MA. S. 50
(FORM G, First schedule to the Marriage Act)

To the registrar of marriages for the _____ district in _____

I hereby give you notice that a marriage is intended to be had within three months from the date hereof at—between me, the undersigned, and the other party herein named.

Name	Condition	Occupation, rank or profession	Age	Dwelling or place of abode	Consent if any
Bride groom, A.B	Bachelor or widower (as case may be)	Merchant (as case may be)			
Bride, C.D	Spinster or widow (as case may be)	Dress maker (as case may be)			Father or Guardian

Witness my hand this _____ day of _____ 20 _____

_____
Signature

APPENDIX 8

REGISTRAR'S CERTIFICATE (foreign marriages)—MA. S.52
(FORM H, First schedule to the Marriage Act)

I, _____, a registrar of marriages for _____ district, do hereby certify that on the _____ day of _____ 20 _____ notice was duly entered in the marriage notice book at _____ of the marriage intended between the parties herein named and described.

Such notice being delivered under the hand of _____ one of the parties, whose usual place of abode for one week immediately preceding the date of such notice had been at _____ in this district, that is to say:

Name	Condition	Occupation, rank or profession	Age	Dwelling or place of abode	Consent, if any and by whom given
A.B.	Bachelor	Merchant (as case may be			
C.D.	Spinster	Dressmaker (as case may be)			Father (as case may be)

If another period has been substituted for the period of one week under the provisions of section 50, alter accordingly.

And I further certify that the said notice has been published in manner provided by the Marriage Act and that I am unaware of any impediment which should obstruct the solemnization of the marriage.

No caveat has been entered against the issue of this certificate; or a caveat was entered against the issue of this certificate on the _____ day of _____ 20 _____ but it has been cancelled.

Witness my hand this _____ day of _____ 20 _____

_____
Registrar of Marriage

APPENDIX 9

MARRIAGE BY NATIVE LAW AND CUSTOM
DECLARATION FORM

I (We) _____ parent(s) (guardians) being the rightful custodians of _____ (woman) and the proper person(s) to receive dowry and give consent to a marriage contracted by her according to this Native Law and Custom, do hereby declare that _____ (intending husband) has paid full dowry on behalf of _____ (woman) and has fulfilled the requirements of Native Law and Custom and has therefore contracted a native Marriage with _____ (woman) as is permitted by article 35 of the Marriage Ordinace.

In testimony of my (our) declaration of consent to this marriage, I (we) hereunder affix my (our) signature (s) (mark).

Signed _____   Date _____

Before me _____ (Priest or delegate)

I have explained the meaning of the above to the parent(s) (guardians) and he/she/they seemed to understand the meaning of it and signified her/his/their agreement willingly.
Signed _____
Parish _____

APPENDIX 10

PETITION FOR DECREE OF DISSOLUTION OF MARRIAGE, NULLITY OF MARRIAGE OR JUDICIAL SEPARATION—
MCR-Order5, Rules 11,18 & 23
(FORM 6, First schedule to the Matrimonial Causes Rules 1983)

(Title)
To the above named High Court.
The petitioner, whose address is _____ and whose occupation is _____, petitions the court for a decree of _____ against the respondent, whose address is _____ and whose occupation is _____, on the ground of _____

MARRIAGE

1   The petitioner, then a (conjugal condition), was lawfully married to (or went through a ceremony of marriage with) the respondent, then a (conjugal condition), at _____ on the _____ day of _____ 20 _____, according to Christian rites.

2   The surname of the _____ immediately before the marriage (or purported marriage) was

3   (Insert any further particulars see sub-rule (5) or (6) of Order V, rule 1)

BIRTH OF PETITIONER AND RESPONDENT

4   The petitioner was born at _____ on the day of _____ 20 _____ and the respondent was born at _____ on the day of _____ 20 _____

5   (Insert any particular require by sub rule (2) of Order V, rule 2)

DOMICILE OR RESIDENCE

6 The petitioner is, within the meaning of Act, domiciled in Nigeria. The facts on which the court will be asked to find that the petitioner is so domiciled are as follows-

COHABITATION

7 Particulars of the places at which and periods during which the petitioner and the respondent have cohabited are as follows-

Or

7 The petitioner and respondent have never cohabited.

8 The date on which and circumstances in which cohabitation between the petitioner and respondent ceases (or last ceased) are as follow—(Leave out if the petitioner and respondent have never cohabited).

CHILDREN

9 There are no children to whom Order V rule 5 applies

Or

9 Particulars relating to the children to whom Order V rule 8 applies are as follows-

PREVIOUS PROCEEDINGS

10 Since the marriage (or ceremony of marriage) there have not been any previous proceedings in a court between the petitioner and the respondent.

Or

10 he following are particulars of previous proceedings between the petitioner and the respondent since the marriage (or ceremony of marriage)

11 Since the marriage (or ceremony of marriage) there have not been any proceedings, instituted otherwise than between the parties to the marriage, concerning the maintenance, custody, guardianship, welfare, advancement or education of a child of the marriage.

Or

11 The following are the particulars of proceedings that have been instituted since the marriage (or ceremony of marriage), otherwise than between the parties to the marriage, concerning the maintenance, custody, guardianship, welfare, advancement or education of a child of the marriage-

FACTS

12 The facts relied on by the petitioner as constituting the ground specified above are as follows-

CONDONATION, CONNIVANCE AND COLLUSION
(Leave out in the case of a petition for nullity of marriage.)

13 The petitioner has not condoned or connived at the ground (or any of the grounds) specified above, and is not guilty of collusion in presenting this petition.

13 The petitioner has not connived at the ground (or any of the grounds) specified above, and is not guilty of collusion in presenting this petition. The following facts are furnished in relation to condonation—

PROPOSED ARRANGEMENTS FOR CHILDREN
(Leave out if Order V, rule 14 does not apply.)

14 (Here state the matters required by Order V, rule 14.)

MAINTENANCE AND SETTLEMENT OF PROPERTY

(Leave out if no order for maintenance or settlement of property is sought)

15 (Here set out the particulars require by Order XIV, rule 4.)

EXERCISE OF COURTS DISCRETION

(Leave out if Order V, rule 13A does not apply)

15 The Court will be asked to make a decree notwithstanding the facts and circumstances set out in the discretion statement filed herewith.

OTHER MATTERS

(In the succeeding paragraphs set out any additional matters, including any matters required or permitted to be stated by virtue of Order V, rule 15 or 21 or Order XIV, rule 4.)

ORDERS SOUGHT

The petitioner seeks the following orders-

(a) A decree of _____ on the ground of _____
(b) (In the following sub-paragraphs set out each other sought)

This petition was settled by (name of Counsel.)

Legal practitioner for the petitioner
Filed on the _____ day of _____ 20 _____ by
_____ on behalf of the petitioner, whose address for service
is _____

CASES

- Agu v Agu (1966), Suit No. E/ID (unreported), Enugu High Court.

- Abisogun v Abisogun, ALL NLR, 1(1963) 237.

- Adegoroye v Adegoroye, NWLR, 2 (1996), Pt. 712.

- Adepeju v Adereti, WNLR, (1961) 154.

- Adeyemi v Bamidele, ALL NLR, (1968), 31, 34.

- Adisatu Awero v Olajida Ishola, (1962) Case No. B/229/62, Grade "B"

- C.C.Egba Odeda.

- Agongo v Aseleke & ors., NMLR, (1961), 21.

- Akparanta v Akparanta, ECLSR, 2(1972), pt., 779.

- Akuwudike v Akuwudike, ENLR, 7(1963), 5,6.

- Alfa v Arepo, WNLR, (1963), 95.

- Anyaegbunam v Anyaegbunam, SC, 4 (1973), 121.

- Ashiv v Agbende, FNR, 1(1976), 216.

- Beamish v beamish, HL, 9(1959-1961), pt.330.

- Beckley v Abiodun, NLR, 17(1943), 59.

- Bhojwani v Bhojwani, NWLR, 6(1996), pt., 457.

- Bolatito v Albert, B (1960)Grade B C.C, Ilesha suit no.UB/21/60.

- Corbett v Corbett, WLR, 2(1970),1308.

- DeReneville v DeReneville, ALL ER, 1(1948),56.

- Dejonwo v Dejonwo, NWLR, 1(1993), pt., 306.

- Dura Aonde v Yomekaa Agoii (1981) Benue High Court, suit no.

- GBB/32A/1981.

- Eshugbayi Eleko v Government of Nigeria, AC, (1931), 662.

- Estate of Agboruja—Deceased, NLR, (1949),38.

- Head v Cox, ALL ER, 1(1964), 776.

- Hyde v Hyde, LRPD, (1886), 133.

- Igbokwe v U.C.H Board of Management, WNLR, (1961), 173.

- Ikedingwu v Okafor, ENLR, (1966),178.

- J.C. Egwu v Meribe, SC, 3(1976), 23.

- Kpelanya v Tsoka and anor., NMLR, (1971), 86.

- Lawal v Younan, WNLR,(1959), 155.

- Lewis v Bankole, NLR, 1(1908), 81.

- Martins v Adenuga, NLR, 18(1964), 63.

- Nwafia v Ububa, NMLR, (1966), 219.

- Obasi & ors v Obasi, ISLR,(1979), 558

- Obele Iliya v Obele, NMLR, 1(1973), pt. 155.

- Obiekwe v Obiekwe, ENLR, 7(1963), 196.

- Okeke v Okeke & ors (1966),(unreported), Onitsha High Court, Suit no.

- O/26N1965 of 28/3/66.

- Okpakapa v Okor and anor, (unreported) Lagos High Court, suit no.

- LD/634/1969.

- Osamwonyi v Osamwonyi, SC, 10(1972), 1.

- Owonyin v Omotosho, ALL NLR, (1961), 304.

- Owobiyi v Owobiyi, ALL NLR, 2(1965), 200.

- R v Princewell, NNLR, (1963), 54.

- Rotibi v. Savage, NLR, 17(1944), 77.

- Runbelow v Runbelow, ALL ER, 2(1965), 767.

- Shashie v Salako (1976) INMLR 160.

- Towoyemi v Towoyemi, NWLR, 7(2001), pt. 702.

- Ugboma v Morah, NLR, (1940), 78.

Sources and Bibliography

SOURCES

- *Acta Apostolicae Sedis*: Commentarium Officiale, Rome: Typis Polygolttis vaticanis, 1929—

- *Acta Sanctae Sedis*, Romae: Typographia Polyglota S.C. de Propaganda Fide, 41 vols. 1865-1909.

- *Acta Synodalia Sacrosancti Concilii Oecumenici Vaticani 11*, (Congregationes Generales), 4 vols. Rome: Typis Polyglottis Vaticanis, 1970-1978.

- *Codex Juris Canocici*, Auctoritate Benedicti XV Promulgatus, May 27, 1917: AAS 9 (1917) II, 11-456.

- *Codex Juris Canonici*, Auctoritate Joannis Pauli II Promulgatus, January 25, 1983: AAS 75 (1983) II, 1-301.

- *Codicis Juris Canonici Fontes*, ed. Gasparri, P. & Seredi, J., vols. 1-10, Romae: Typis Polyglottis Vaticanis, 1923-1939.

- *Collectaea S. Congregationis de Propaganda Fide*, Romae: Typographis Polyglotta S.C. de Propagamda Fide, 2 Vols, 1891-1907.

- *Concilium Tridentinum, Diariorum, Actorum, Epistularum, Nova Collectio*, ed., Societas Goerresiana, St. Louis: Herder, 1901-1938.

- *Exegetical Commentary on the Code of Canon Law*, eds., Marzoa J., Miras J., & Rodriguez-Ocana R., 8vols, Montreal: Wilson & Lafleur, 2004.

- Mansi, J., *sacrorum Conciliorum Nova et Amplissima Collectio*, Paris, 1901-1927.

- Migne, J.P., *Patrologiae Cursus Completus, Series Graeca*, Paris, 1857-1866.

- _____, *Patrologiae Cursus Completus, Series Latina*, Paris, 1844-1866.

- *Pontificia Commissio Codici Juris Canonici Recognoscendo, Communicationes,* Romae: Typis Polyglottis Vaticanis, *1969*-1983.

- *Sacrae Romanae Rotae Decisiones seu Sententiae Quae prodierunt ab anno 1909,* Rome: Typis Polyglottis Vaticanis, 1912—

- Richter-Schulte, *Canones et Decreta Concilii Tridentini,* Leipzig, 1853.

- Sanctissimi Domini Nostri Benedicti Papae XIV, *Bullarium,* ed. Recentior auctior et emendatior, Venice, 1768.

- _____ *De Synodo Diocesano,* Rome, Typographia, S.C. de P.F., 1806.

- *The Holy Bible* (The Jerusalem bible), London: Darton Longman & Todd Ltd, 1968.

- *The Catechism of the Catholic Church*, Ibadan: Pauline publications, 1994.

- *Vatican Council II: The conciliar and post conciliar documents*, Austin. F.(ed), Northport, New York: Costello publishing co., 1975.

- *Western Region of Nigeria Laws, 1959*, Criminal Code, cap. 28; customary Court Laws, cap. 31; High court Law, cap.44.

- *Laws of Eastern Nigeria, 1963*, Limitation of Dowry Law, cap. 76.

- *Laws of Nothern Nigeria, 1963*, The Sharia Court of Appeal Law, cap. 122; Native Authority Law, cap. 77; High court Law, cap. 49; Native Courts Law, cap. 18.

- *Laws of the Federation and Lagos*, 1958, the State Court (Federal Jurisdiction) Act, cap. 177.

- *Laws of the Federation of Nigeria, 1990*, The Marriage Act, cap. 218; The Matrimonial causes Act and rules, cap.220; The Criminal Code, cap.77; The Evidence Act, cap.112; The Nigeria Interpretation Act, 1964, cap. 192.

- *Laws of Nigeria, 1971, Marriage (Appointment of Principal Registrar, Registrars etc) Notice, no.72; Marriage (Designation of Districts) Order, no.73; Marriage (Location of Marriage Offices) Direction, no.74.*

- *The New Catholic Encyclopaedia, University of Chicago press, Chicago, vols 5 & 9, 1990.*

- *The constitutions of the Federal Republic of Nigeria, a compendium, 1963, 1979 & 1999.*

REFERENCE WORKS

- ABATE, A.M., "Gli impedimenti matrimoniali nel nuovo codice di diritto canonico," in *Apollinaris,* 60(1987), p. 501.

- _____, "L'Assistenza con facolta supplica," in *Il Matrimonio nella nuova legislazione canonica,* Roma: 1984, pp. 144-148.

- ABBASS, J.A., *Two Codes in Comparison,* Rome: Pontificio Istituto Orientale,1997.

- ABBO, J.A., "The form of marriage," in *Priest,* 20 (1964), pp. 64-66.

- ADESANYA, S.A., *Law of Matrimonial causes,* Ibadan: Ibadan University Press, 1973.

- ADERIBIGBE, R.M. *Family Law in Nigeria,* Lagos: Godas Publishing Consult, 2004.

- AGUDA, T.A., ed., *Marriage Laws in Nigeria,* Lagos: The Nigerian Institute of Advanced Legal Studies, 1981.

- ALESANDRO, J., "Marriage Legislation in The New Code," in CLSA, *Proceedings of the forty-second annual convention of the canon law society of America,* Washington, D.C.: 1980, pp. 87-89.

- AZNAR-GIL, F.R., *El Nuevo Derecho Matrimonial Canonico,* 2nd ed., Universidad Pontificia Salamanca, 1985.

- BERSINI, F., *Il Nuovo Diritto Canonico Matrimoniale,* 3rd ed., Turin: Elle Di Ci., 1985.

- BERSINI, F., "Errore commune e assistenza al matrimonio," in *Monitor Ecclesiasticus*, 99 (1974), pp. 89-111

- BONNET, P.A. & GULLO, C. (eds.), *Diritto matrimoniale canonico (Vol. III)*, Libreria editrice vaticana, Città del Vaticano 2002-2005.

- BOUSCAREN, T.L., *The Canon Law Digest*, Milwaukee: Bruce Publishing Co., 1934-1983.

- BUCCI, O., "La famiglia nella prassi giuridica e nella vita dei Cristiani Orientali," in *Utrumque ius*, 16 (1987), pp. 123-124

- CASTANO, J.F., "Dispenza dagli impedimenti e della forma canonica nell' attuale codice di Diritto Canonico," in *Angelicum*, 70 (1985), pp. 395ff.

- CASTELLO, J., *Domicile and quasi-domicile*, Washington: Catholic University, 1930.

- CORBETT, P.E., *The Roman Law of Marriage*, Oxford: Clarendon press, 1930.

- CORIDEN, A.J.-GREEN, J.T.-HEINTSCHEL, E.D., (eds), *The Code of Canon Law: A Text and Commentry*, Geoffrey Chapman, London, 1985.

- CORECCO, E., "Dimettersi della Chiesa per ragioni fiscali" in *Apollinaris*, 55(1982), p. 470f.

- D'AURIA, A., *Il Matrimonio nel Diritto della Chiesa*, Rome: Lateran University Press, 2003.

- DUNDERDALE, E., "Canonical Form of Marriage: Anachronism or Pastoral Necessity," in *Studia Canonica*, 12 (1978), pp. 41-45.

- ELIAS, T.O., *The nature of African Customary Law*, London: Manchester University press, 1956.

- —————, *Groundwork of Nigeria Law*, London: Routledge & Kegan Paul, 1954.

- EPISCOPAL CONFERENCE OF NIGERIA, *Particular complementry norms to the Revised Code*, Lagos, 1989.

- FRANCESCHI, H., *Riconocimento e tutela dello "ius connubii" nel sistema matrimoniale canonico*, Milano: Giuffrè editore, 2004.

- FARIS, J.D., "Canonical issues in the pastoral care of Eastern Catholics," in CLSA, *Proceedings of the fifty-third Annual convention, San Antonio, Texas, October 14-17, 1991*, Washington D.C: 1992, p. 164ff.

- GARNER, B.A., et al (eds), *Black's Law Dictionary*, 7th ed., Minnesota: West Publishing co., 1999.

- GASPARRI, P., *Tractatus Canonicus de Matrimonio*, Città del Vaticano: Typis Polyglottis Vaticanis, 1932.

- GEFAELL, P., "commentary to the Spanish "Orientaciones", n. 29 in *Ius Ecclesiae*, 18 (2006), no. 3, p. 846.

- GIL, F., *The form of marriage in the code of canon law and the code of canons of the Eastern Churches*, Canon Law Studies, Washington, D.C.: CUA Press, 1995.

- GOLDSMITH, J.W., "The Competence of Church and State over Marriage—Disputed points," in *The Jurist*, 6 (1946), pp. 195-201.

- GOVE, P.B., (ed.), *Webster's third new International dictionary*, Cologne: K:V:MBH publishers, 1993.

- HERVADA, J., *Studi sull'essenza della matrimonio*, Milano: Giuffrè editore, 2000.

- HUBNER, R., *History of Germanic Private Law*, Boston: Little Brown & co., 1918.

- HUGHES, M., "The Juridical nature of joining the Catholic Church." in *Studia Canonica*, 8 (1974), n.1, pp. 45ff.

- JOYCE, G.H., *Christian Marriage: An Historical and doctrinal study*, London: Sheed & Ward, 1948.

- KASUMU, A.B.-SALACUSE, J.W., *Nigeria Family Law*, London: Butterworths, 1966.

- LEWIN, J., *Studies in African Native Law*, Cape Town: The African Bookman, 1947.

- LYNCH, J.E., "The Eastern Churches: Historical background" in *The Jurist*, 51(1991), pp. 1-17.

- MARTI, F., "Un commento alla lettera circolare del PCTL del 13 Marzo 2006", in *Ius Eccesiae*, 19 (2007), no. 1, pp. 247-267.

- MCMANUS, F.R., "Marriage in the canons of the Eastern Catholic Churches" in *The Jurist*, 54 (1994), pp.63f.

- MURPHY, F.X., *Synod '67*, Milwaukee: the Bruce publishing co., 1967.

- NAVARRETE, U., "De ministro sacramenti matrimonii in Ecclesia Latina et Ecclesiis Orientalibus tentamen explicationis concordatis" in *Periodica*, 84 (1995), pp. 711-733.

- NEUFELD, E., *Ancient Hebrew Marriage Laws*, New York: Longmans, 1944.

- NEDUNGATT, G., "Minister of the Sacrament of marriage in the East and the West," in *Periodica* 90 (2001), 305-388.

- NWOGUGU, E.I., *Family Law in Nigeria*, Ibadan: Heinemann Education Books, 1990.

- OBI, S.N.C., *Modern Family Law in Southern Nigeria*, London: Sweet & Maxwell, 1966.

- _____, *The Customary Law Manual*, Enugu: Government Press, 1977.

- OBILADE, A.O., *The Nigerian Legal System*, Ibadan: Spectrum books ltd., 2001.

- OKPALOKA, P., *Legal Protection of Marriage and the family institutions*, Onitsha: Trinitas publications, 2002.

- ONOKAH, M.C., *Family Law*, Ibadan: Spectrum Books Limited, 2003.

- ÖRSY, L., "Christian Marriage: Doctrine and Law," in *The Jurist*, 40 (1980), pp. 282-348.

- ORTIZ, M.A., "Sezione IV—La forma della celebrazione (1108-1123; 1130-1133). Cap. 1. La forma (cann. 1108-1110; 1114-1115; 1117-1123)", in BONNET, P.A. & GULLO, C. (eds.), *Diritto matrimoniale canonico (Vol. III)*, Libreria editrice vaticana, Città del Vaticano 2002-2005, pp. 25-56.

- PASTOR, L. von, *The History of the Popes*, ed. Ralph F.K, 40 vols., Louis: B. Herder books co., 1928-1953.

- PINTO, P.V. (ed.), *Commento al Codice dei canoni delle Chiese orientali*, Vatican City: Libreria Editrice Vaticana, 2001.

- PIVONKA, L.P., "Ecumenical or Mixed Marriage in the New Code of Canon Law," in *The Jurist*, 43 (1983), pp. 103-124.

- POMPEDDA, M.F., *Studi di diritto matrimoniale canonico*, Milano: Giuffrè editore, 2002.

- POSPISHIL, V.J., *Eastern Catholic Marriage Law According to the Code of Canons of the Eastern Churches*, Brooklyn, NY: Saint Maron Publications, 1991.

- ——————, *Eastern Catholic Church Law*, Staten Island, NY: Saint Maron Publications, 1996.

- POSPISHIL, V.J. & FARIS, J.D., *The New Latin code of canon law and Eastern Catholics*, Brooklyn, NY: Saint Maron publications, 1984.

- PRADER, J., *Il matrimonio in Oriente e in Occidente*, Rome: Pontificio Istituto Orientale, 2003.

- ROBERSON, R., *The Eastern Christian Churches: A brief survey*, 6th edition, Rome: Orientalia Christiana, 1999.

- RUTHERFORD, L., & BONE, S. (eds.), *Osborn's Concise Law Dictionary*, London: Sweet & Maxwell, 1993.

- SALACHAS, D., *Il sacramento del matrimonio nel nuovo dirito canonico delle Chiese Orientali*, Roma: Edizioni Dehoniane, 1994.

- SCHULZ, F., *Classical Roman law*, Oxford: Clarendon Press, 1961.

- SHERMAN, C., *Roman law in the modern world*, 2nd ed., New York: Baker Voorhis & co., 1924.

- STENSON, A., "The concept and implications of the formal act of defection, canon 1117" in *Studia Canonica*, 21 (1987), pp. 189ff.

- WOYWOD, "Obligation of Pastor to Examine and Instruct Parties Before Marriage," in *The Homiletic and Pastoral Review*, 37 (1937), pp. 744-745.

TABLE OF CONTENTS OF THE COMPLETE THESIS

SECTION TWO: FORM OF MARRIAGE FROM THE
COUNCIL OF TRENT TO THE PRESENT TIME
    1.1.1 The Council of Trent and the promulgation of the
        decree *Tametsi*
    1.1.2 The Benedictine declaration and other
        dispensations from the decree *Tametsi*
    1.2.3 The decree *Ne Temere*
    1.2.4 The 1917 code on the canonical form of marriage
    1.2.5 The interventions between 1918 and 1963
    1.2.6 The Vatican II council on the form of marriage
    1.2.7 The legislations on the form of marriage from the
        Vatican II council to the 1983 code

CHAPTER TWO: THE CURRENT CANONICAL NORMS ON THE FORM OF MARRIAGE

SECTION ONE: CANONICAL FORM IN THE 1983
LATIN CODE
    2.1.1 The Preliminary formalities
    2.1.2 The ordinary form
        2.1.2.1 The official witness
            2.1.2.1.1 The local ordinary
            2.1.2.1.2 The parish priest
            2.1.2.1.3 The legitimately and validly
                delegated priest or deacon
            2.1.2.1.4 The legitimately and validly
                delegated lay person
            2.1.2.1.5 The supply of faculty in
                cases of doubt and error
            2.1.2.1.6 The basis of faculty of the
                official witness
        2.1.2.2 The common witnesses
        2.1.2.3 The manner of assisting by the witnesses
    2.1.3 Persons bound by the canonical form

www.ingramcontent.com/pod-product-compliance
Lightning Source LLC
Chambersburg PA
CBHW020522290526

45786CB00002B/719